A Walk in
Fields of Gold

Published by Spiral Press, R.R. 5 Rockwood, ON Canada N0B 2K0

www.spiralpress.ca

Cover photograph by Richard Goodship

Library and Archives Canada Cataloguing in Publication

   A walk in fields of gold : an anthology of prose & poetry / Headwaters Writers' Guild.

ISBN 978-0-9681981-9-3

   1. Canadian literature (English)—Ontario—Orangeville.
2. Canadian literature (English)—21st century.
I. Nye, Gloria, II. Headwaters Writers' Guild

PS8257.O73W35 2010   C810.8'006   C2010-906775-4

10 9 8 7 6 5 4 3 2

A Walk in
Fields of Gold

An Anthology
of Prose & Poetry

Headwaters Writers' Guild

Spiral
Press

Rockwood, ON

"And by the way, everything in life is writable about if you have the outgoing guts to do it, and the imagination to improvise. The worst enemy to creativity is self-doubt."
~ *Sylvia Plath*

Dedicated to the memory of
past members

Ed Wildman

Janet Bellinger

and

Len Rich

"If there's a book you really want to read, but it hasn't been written yet, then you must write it."
~ Toni Morrison

Table of Contents

"The best time for planning a book is while you're doing the dishes."
~ *Agatha Christie*

INTRODUCTION
TO HEADWATERS WRITERS' GUILD

After I read an article about Ed Wildman—lawyer, writer, poet and writing instructor—I carried his phone number in my wallet for months. He mentioned that he wanted to write novels but at the moment he was writing poetry. Since I wanted to write novels and I'd been writing poetry, I'd thought that Ed would understand. And I hoped his workshops would help me write. I wasn't mistaken.

At the first workshop on October 25, 2001, Ed explained that he'd taken a course from Natalie Goldberg, author of *Writing Down the Bones*, in Taos, New Mexico. He assured us that if we followed her methods we'd never have writer's block again.

In Ed's workshops, he always found something positive to say about everybody's writing. We all wanted to wow him. He always inspired or encouraged us to do our best. "You can never be defeated unless you quit," Ed said.

For two years, Janet Bellinger and I attended Ed's weekly workshops in Honeywood. Sometimes, unable to attend the workshops due to bad weather, we'd write together at a coffee shop in Orangeville. Janet often said, "Wouldn't it be great if we had a writing group in Orangeville?" Janet planted the seed for the formation of the Headwaters Writers' Guild.

When Ed stopped having his workshops in 2003, I began having withdrawal pains. I tried to coerce Ed to continue, but to no avail. After many emails, on December 9, 2003, three members from Ed's workshops met upstairs at the Orangeville Library and we followed the same format as Ed's workshops.

On December 30, 2003, Ed became a member of our writing group. We were ecstatic. He remained a member until he died on June

20, 2004. The five of us mourned him and, for years, we kept an empty chair for him.

Presently, we have approximately twenty-six members with an average of twelve to sixteen people attending our twice-a-month meetings.

At our meetings, we continue to follow Ed's format, writing from prompts and sharing our raw writing. We also bring our work in progress or completed work to read. One of our purposes is to inspire and encourage one another, so positive and constructive feedback is welcome.

We're a diverse group of writers who write fiction, non-fiction, magazine articles, newspaper columns and poetry. Members vary from beginners to published writers with everyone sharing their expertise. We delight in our members' successes and it's gratifying to see how much we've accomplished. In 2003, we were all beginning writers who were writing to find our voices. Now, many of our members have published books, articles, short stories and even *Words Aloud* winning poetry.

As with Ed's writing workshops, we are an open group and we welcome all writers or people who long to write.

Our website at www.headwaterswritersguild.com has information about our meetings.

For personal input from our members, go to our blog at: www.headwaterswritersguild.blogspot.com.

Janet Bellinger, a founding member of the Headwaters Writers' Guild, passed away in October 2007. When I wrote with Janet, I did the best writing of my life. The muse always arrived for us, and we were passionate about writing. Janet and I wrote every day and, in the beginning of our friendship, we shared our writing by email. She was always a staunch supporter of mine and inspired me to continue writing.

Len Rich, an award-winning author and photographer who mentored all of us, died in April, 2009. When Len, who was a published author, joined our writing group, most of our members were impressed. I was puzzled why he wanted to join a group of beginning writers, so I asked him. With a twinkle in his eyes and a smile, he said, "I have a wealth of knowledge that I'd like to share with other writers. I could help them." Without Len's help, I would never have written my first published article.

We have dedicated this anthology to the memories of Ed Wildman, Janet Bellinger, and Len Rich.

I'd like to think that Ed, Janet and Len write together and they still mentor us from heaven. I miss my friends and writing buddies.

In an email to me on April 6, 2004, Ed said that he hoped that we would pass on what we learned to others. I believe we succeeded, although there will never be another Ed Wildman.

Nancy Rorke
Founding Member
njd411@yahoo.com

"The pages are still blank, but there is a miraculous feeling of the words being there, written in invisible ink and clamoring to become visible."
~ Vladimir Nabakov

> *"It seems to me that those songs*
> *that have been any good,*
> *I have nothing much to do with the writing of them.*
> *The words have just crawled down my sleeve*
> *and come out on the page."*
> *~ Joan Baez*

Diane Bator

Diane moved from Alberta to Orangeville with her husband, three kids and a cat. She chose to bloom where she's been planted and has rekindled her passions for writing and painting. She joined the Headwaters group in April, 2007 and has written several novels, short stories and poems that await publication. She has been published in *Mid-Bits Magazine, Stories of Prayers and Faith,* and has written song lyrics for her father Joe Rondeau, a musician in Alberta. She has held a variety of interesting jobs but loves hanging out with her kids the best.

FALSE TEETH

Being a bank teller is a lot like being a bartender. People come in and tell you things you never thought you would hear. Half the time, they leave you shaking your head and wanting a drink. Take Mr. Wampole—a customer since we used animal hides as currency. He was also our mailman.

On a Monday full of problems, I had just returned from lunch when I saw his sour face glowering at me across the reception desk. A headache throbbed in the back of my brain and I was an inch away from running out the back door, screaming. I faked a smile and asked, "How can I help you today, Mr. Wampole?"

"You can help me by finding my teeth," he said.

"Your teeth?" My jaw dropped and I sat up straight in my chair.

"Yeah. I think they fell out this morning while I was doing my route."

I blinked and covered my mouth with the backs of my fingers. This had to be a joke. My lips pressed together as I tried not to laugh. I failed miserably and, with a snort, burst into giggles.

"Okay, who put you up to this?" I asked. "Was it the girls in mid-office?"

Mr. Wampole stared at me, working his lips like he was about to say something. His hands clenched the back of the chair in front of him.

My laughter trailed off when I noticed his frown. "You're serious."

He nodded.

My cheeks burned.

"I'm so sorry," I said. "I really thought you were joking."

He opened his mouth to bare his empty lower jaw. Over the years, nature had knocked out most of his teeth and dentists had sold him two lumpy pieces of plastic to chew with. One plate was missing. "Does this look like a joke, missy?"

I stammered another apology and jotted down his name and phone number. "We'll call you if your teeth turn up."

Muttering under his breath, he shook his head and left the bank. He probably thought I was the most addle-brained person he had ever met. After my fit of giggles, I can't say I blamed him.

I scurried out of my seat and ran around the low wall into mid-office. "Did you hear that? Mr. Wampole came in looking for his false teeth. Why on earth would he think we had his dentures?"

Juanita glanced up from her paperwork. "Was it a lower plate?"

I stared at her with my mouth hanging open. "Yes. How did you know?"

"Oh, good." She smiled and asked, "Did you give them to him?"

"Did I give what to him?"

Her brow furrowed. "The teeth. They were behind the photo on the reception desk, wrapped in tissues."

I didn't hear the rest of what she said. I ran back to the front desk and searched for the picture frame. Shoving it to one side, I spied a mass of white tissues. Using only my fingertips, I opened them to reveal one lower dental plate.

"Holy cow," I said. My face grew warm.

"Did you find them?" Juanita walked around the corner.

"Yes."

"Good. Whose did you say they were?"

I winced. "Mr. Wampole's."

"Well, you'd better phone him and let him know they're here," she said.

My eyes darted from teeth to phone. That was one call I was not looking forward to. I was sure he didn't currently think very much of me.

"Who brought the teeth in?" I asked.

"Jack."

"Jack?" That got my attention. Jack Everett was a notorious prankster. Suddenly I was not so sure the whole story rang true. Hearing Jack was involved convinced me further that it was a joke.

Juanita waved her hand toward the window. "He said that he pulled into the parking lot and nearly stepped on them when he got out of his truck. He brought them inside so I rinsed them off and wrapped them up. "

Good for him, I thought. I probably wouldn't have dared touch them. It made me cringe just to touch the tissues.

I called Mr. Wampole who returned to the bank in eight minutes flat.

"Good thing you caught me," he said. "I was just leaving Price Chopper and heading for Shelburne. Those darn teeth don't fit very well and I was taking them in to get fixed."

"So they just fell out?" I asked.

"Nah, I put them down on the seat and must have knocked them out when I pulled out the mail. First time I've ever knocked my own teeth out." He grinned, baring his empty lower jaw.

I winced and used two fingers to hand him the wad of tissues. "Here you go. Juanita rinsed the dirt off them for you."

Mr. Wampole shook the teeth out of the bundle, letting the tissues drift to the floor. He held them up to the light and studied them. "Yup, those are mine all right."

He rubbed the false teeth against his pant leg and shoved them in his mouth. With a tip of his baseball cap, he walked out the front door into the spring sunshine.

"A story should have a beginning, a middle, and an end . . . but not necessarily in that order."
~ Jean Luc Godard

REALM OF ENDLESS SKY

I dance in the meadow while the sun sets
The periwinkle sky tinged with baby pink clouds
My feet circle through the dying grass
Giving thanks for another perfect day
Beneath the realm of endless sky
As the sky darkens to lavender, I sway
The clouds become rich like raspberry
Someone sets fire to the wood in the circle
Flames devour dried logs and twigs
And still I dance, grasses whispering around me
The sky fades to deep amethyst
The clouds turn burgundy then disappear
As the night wears on, the flames lick the sky
Higher and higher until their tips are out of sight
We sit and tell stories in the glow until dawn
When golden sunrise warms our bodies
We douse the embers and go home.

PETUNIA'S PERIL

Petunia drove along the Monterey Coast Highway looking for the exact spot to complete her mission. She knew the site the instant she saw it and pulled the car to a stop across the wrong side of the road. It didn't matter if she wasn't properly parked on the shoulder, what she needed would only take a minute or two. Besides, she was sure no one ever used this stretch of road so late at night. The curves were too hazardous. She turned off the car lights, just in case, and relied on the light of the full moon.

She got out of the car, being careful where she stepped in her new Manolos. She didn't have the insurance money yet, so they weren't even paid for. Petunia grabbed the gray urn, then sat on the metal guardrail and swung her legs over. One of her heels slid into a crack in the baked earth. She cursed and wiggled out of her shoe before bending down to pry it out.

Unceremoniously, she dumped Martin's ashes over the stone cliff. There were no trees to shield her from the few fragments that blew back into the car. She wiped some off her face. She brushed what she could off her clothes and wrinkled her nose. Her gaze followed the rest of his particles as they wafted through the salty air before dropping to the pounding waves below.

Petunia smiled. The miniscule parts of the late Martin Theodore would settle among the boulders and be impossible to separate from the rest of the dirt.

Her blouse, damp with sweat, clung to her curves. She smelled like she had run a marathon rather than attended her husband's funeral. She didn't care. He was gone and she just had to wait for the lawyer to settle the estate before she left the West Coast for good.

When they first met, Martin had been one of those men who bought flowers and rubbed her tired feet after a hard day of shopping. He bought her glittering trinkets and treated her like a princess. Hell, didn't they all at first?

Time went on, as it tends to do, and within two years things changed. She discovered Martin was a workaholic. He stopped going to the gym and lost most of the muscle tone he had when she met him. Petunia was repulsed by his sagging body and did not let him touch her after their first anniversary, in case sloth was a contagious condition.

Once their second anniversary hit, they hardly spoke to each other and she moved his belongings into the guest room. Martin wanted her to grow up and get a life of her own. She was trapped and needed to get out of the loveless marriage, but she also wanted half of the vast fortune he had willed to his first wife and kids. Her only options were to divorce the loser . . . or kill him.

The pool boy had made the second option become the most logical one when he knocked his boom box—plugged into an outlet at the time—into the pool last month while he was skimming it.

"Are you stupid? Don't you know that thing could have electrocuted someone?" Petunia asked. "I'm docking you a day's pay for that."

The pool boy shrugged. "Your husband won't do that. He'll say it was an accident. Besides, no one was in the pool so no harm done."

"But I could have been." She glared at him with her hands on her hips.

"You would never go in the water if there was anything floating in it. That's why I have to come here every morning so you can swim. You're nothing but a spoiled trophy wife who can't do anything except spend other people's money."

"You can't talk to me like that," she said. "I'll have you fired."

He shrugged. "Lady, you don't sign my paycheques, your husband does."

"He'll fire you if I ask him to."

"I've been with him ten years," the pool boy said. "You've been here for two. I've seen better women than you come and go, so who do you think he'll get rid of first?"

Petunia walked off in a huff. The more she thought about the possibility of electrocution, the bigger her smile grew. When he was ready to leave, she—wearing nothing more than a string bikini and a flimsy silk sarong—met him at his truck.

"I'm sorry for my outburst earlier," she said. "Why don't you come back up to the house for a drink? We can sit in the hot tub and talk this over."

The pool boy's dark eyes narrowed. "What about your husband?"

"He's in South America for two more days."

He grinned, then put his tools into the truck and walked toward the house with her. That was how she was able to test her theory. With thousands of able-bodied young men in Los Angeles, who would miss one pool boy? Besides, she was young and strong. It had been easy for her to bury him beneath the rose bushes.

Her face fell.

The boom box had been the weapon in two murders so she had no choice except to get rid of it. Petunia groaned. The ends of the guardrail were too far to walk around in killer heels, so she sat on the metal and swung her legs over the top again. She yanked open the passenger door of the BMW and grabbed the boom box. Since it was too heavy for her to toss from the car, she set it on the guardrail and realized that she would have to climb back over the guardrail in order for it to go over the cliff.

Cursing beneath her breath, she dropped the boom box to the other side, then climbed over the guardrail yet again. As she straightened up, her heel caught in another crack in the dry ground. This time, she ignored it. There was more work to be done.

Petunia tossed the boom box over the cliff after Martin's ashes. She watched it soar through the air and shatter on the rocks, exactly the way she thought it would.

She smiled. The sea air cooled her sweaty body and refreshed her. Petunia lifted her arms to let her shirt dry out. She glanced down and noticed a smudge on her skirt. Wiping it off, she hoped to hell it wasn't some small tell-tale bit of Martin. She hated wearing funeral black since it showed the dust so easily, but it was part of the package and people would expect to see her wearing it to mourn. At least they had with her last husband.

Larry's death had been just as easy to orchestrate. He was an avid gardener and she was smart enough to pay attention when he rambled on about arsenic in the fertilizers and cyanide in the rat poison. She showed him who the real rat was.

It was too late now. There was nothing anyone could do to prove either man's death had been anything but an accident. They were both cremated and she particularly liked this desolate spot to scatter their ashes. No one ever paid attention to anyone who stopped to enjoy the view . . . or dispose of evidence.

Petunia tugged the elastic out of her long hair and let it blow free in the night wind. Free. She loved that word. Once she got the insurance money, she would move on to another town and find husband number three.

The ground shifted beneath Petunia's feet and made her take a half-step closer to the cliff. Her breath caught in her throat until she regained her balance. Another damned earthquake. This one had nearly thrown her into the ocean. Only the heel of her shoe, stuck into the crack in the ground, saved her from taking one more step and sliding down the rocky face.

Petunia let out a laugh. How ironic would that have been? She sat on the barrier, ready to climb over and get into her car, but the heel of her shoe wouldn't budge. She bent down to free it, like she had before, sitting on the guardrail again and trying to wiggle her foot free.

The squeal of tires sounded seconds before the crash. A speeding car hit hers. pushing it against the guardrail and knocking her out of her shoes and into a roll. Grasping wildly at bushes, she could grab nothing that would stop her tumbling toward the edge. Closer and closer—rocks and dust tattered her dress with no regard for the designer label inside. Pebbles and grass caught in her hair. It would take an hour in the shower to get all that out. Suddenly, she had more to worry about than clothes and hair. She was in space . . . falling . . . falling . . . falling.

She felt the splatters of sea spray washing away the blood that trickled down the bridge of her nose. Just before her body hit, she caught a glimpse of something glinting in the moonlight like diamonds —a shattered CD from the pool boy's boom box.

It was the last thing Petunia ever saw.

"Write your first draft with your heart.
Re-write with your head."
~ From the movie Finding Forrester

WHEN I DIED

When I died
The stars went out
One by one

When I died
Light became pure
And brilliant

When I died
An angel reached out
And touched my hand

When I died
I woke up again with
Things still undone

When I died
Was when I began
Living again

Janet Bellinger

Janet was a founding member of the Headwaters Writers' Guild and she wrote her first novel, *Eight is Great* in 1992. She is the author of *Teacher on the Run* which was published in October, 2005. She also wrote poetry. Janet lived in Orangeville, Ontario with her husband Mike. She had a daughter Lindsay, a son Leigh, five cats and two dogs. She passed away October, 2007.

YOU ARE A SYMPHONY

You are a symphony
perfectly orchestrated
to enrapture and delight
You are the wind
riffling cosmic hair
You are the sun
warming the face of the world
It's very soul
You are poetry
joy to the soul

You are ice cream
delight anytime
smooth
soothe
cool against the tongue

You are a burst of spring tulips
fresh
refreshing
jumble of hues
touched by early morning dew

You are coffee
jolting the world awake
when it needs to awaken
You are a page in a book
not quite yet turned
You are a newborn baby
innocent
primal
universal
protective instincts
You are you.

*"Metaphors have a way of holding
the most truth in the least space."
~ Orson Scott Card*

FROZEN APPLES

The only photo I have of my father and I together
Is one of us standing outside Convocation Hall
A shadow covers the left side of our faces
I am carrying a dozen red roses in my arms
We are both smiling
I hold his arm with the very tips of my fingers
And stand about a pace behind
He was proud of me that day
I was happy that day
It reminds me of the day that the sun shone down on the frozen
apples.

Another memory culled from the steaming cauldron of
childhood memories
The annual mushroom hunt
Following my father through field and wood as we gathered
puffballs
My father was a puffball other times but I won't go into that
I choose instead to harvest the pearls
What is the point otherwise?
The man who was an almost doctor
I could loll in the arms of dreadful remembrances
But anger and hate is not for me
I've already been there, done that
And as trite is it may be, I've chosen love.

Mary Patricia Bird

Patricia began writing in high school but didn't take it seriously until 14 years ago when a diagnosis of fibromyalgia forced her out of the workforce. She decided to take this window of opportunity to pursue her dream of becoming a published author. She writes poetry and fiction and has been a member of the Headwaters Writers' Guild since 2004. She lives in Orangeville with her husband and two teenage daughters.

THE LETTER

My hand shook as I pulled the letter out of the mailbox. The return address indicated it had come from my father. I recognized his handwriting even after all this time. He'd passed away three years ago but the postmark was dated a year before that.

I stood frozen to the ground as questions flew through my head like bats dive-bombing a backyard pool. Where had this letter been all this time? Why had my father written to me after ten years of silence? Its arrival three years after his death caused my stomach to roll and I felt slightly faint.

How had he found me? Had this note fallen from the heavens like the spitting rain that had begun to fall?

I closed the mailbox and went back inside my house. The letter was the only mail I received that day. I sat down on the hall bench and turned it over and over in my quivering hands, reluctant to unseal the flap. A fear gripped me. What could I fear from a dead man?

When I was sixteen, I announced to my parents that I was pregnant. My mother sat on the sofa, hands twisting in her lap, and said nothing. Worry lines creased her forehead and between her eyes. My father, however, exploded in fury.

"We brought you up better than that. A girl your age should not be having sex."

I hung my head, unable to look at my father, afraid to utter another word. No amount of explaining could fix what had been done.

"Who did this?" my father wanted to know.

"Ryan," I muttered without looking up.

"Ryan Kipling? He and his family moved out of province a month ago."

I was quite aware of that. My heart broke when Ryan's father got the transfer. We agreed to go our separate ways as we clung to each other during our tearful good-bye. I had not dated another boy. My heart still ached for Ryan—and now I was carrying his child. We had made such a clean break of it that I didn't even get an address or phone number.

"Lorraine," my father said to my mother. "Where did the Kiplings move to?"

"I don't know," she whispered through tear-filled eyes.

"Rachel?" He turned back to me.

I looked up at his scarlet face and blazing eyes. The anger I saw was too much to bear. I had always been daddy's little girl, a feeling that had been crushed with the bomb I had dropped. A lump formed in my throat as tears dripped from my eyes onto my cold hands. My straight brown hair hung like curtains, shading me from my father's glare.

"You only have one choice. Get an abortion."

I snapped my head up. "Daddy, no!"

"What do you mean no?" he roared. "Who do you think is going to look after it? Your mother? Not likely. We're past raising babies."

"I'll raise my own baby," I cried.

"You're sixteen years old—still a baby yourself. You know nothing about raising babies. It takes hard work and money—lots of money. I will not support this child. That's Kipling's responsibility and if you don't know where he is, you will have an abortion."

"Daddy!"

"End of discussion."

He turned and thumped up the stairs. The door slam echoed throughout the house.

"Mom?" I looked at her with pleading eyes.

"I'm sorry, Rachel. I don't know what to say."

My tear-filled eyes widened. "You think I should have an abortion?"

"Well—"

I could see the strain in her eyes, the crease in her forehead. She did not believe in abortion, but she could not cross my father. She shook her head and looked away.

"Why can't you stand up to him? For once in your life, why can't you stand behind me?"

"Rachel, that's not fair."

"Fair?" I came to my feet and stood before her, bile rising. "Do you think it's fair to me or the baby just because a condom ripped?" I cradled my tiny baby bump in my hands. I dropped my voice to a whisper. "I know you were pregnant with me when you and Dad got married. I did the math."

My mother's tears flowed freely, her sobs barely audible as she cupped her face in her hands.

"Why didn't you abort me, huh?"

Mother cringed. "It was different back then."

"You won't support me, will you?"

The next day, I called around to a few of Ryan's friends and one of his buddies had an address and phone number. I called Ryan and the next day, I was on a bus bound for Alberta. I never looked back, never told him where I was going and never spoke to my father again.

I telephoned my mother when Brianna was born. She cried and said she wished she could come see us but my father would not allow it. We made arrangements for me to send mail to her through a neighbour. I sent photographs of her granddaughter and Mom sent us cards, gifts and letters. I sent a wedding invitation when I turned eighteen and Ryan and I were preparing to get married. I don't know whether Mom showed it to Dad or not. She just sent the reply card back with an x in the "unable to attend" box. She never mentioned the wedding in her letters but she kept me up-to-date: what all my friends were up to, which neighbours were feuding, but nothing about my dad and, in the last letter I received, she announced her impending death as she battled breast cancer.

I cried. I wanted to run to her with Brianna and Ryan Junior to meet their grandmother, but time ran out. Two days later, Mom's neighbour called to tell me she was gone.

"She talked about you all the time, you know," Mrs. Reid said. "She felt so bad she couldn't watch her grandchildren grow up."

"I know," I sniffed. "She said so in her letter." I paused. "How is my father?"

"He's devastated. He was with your mother right to the end."

Sadness and anger battled in my soul. He supported my mother, but not the child their love had created. I did not go to my mother's funeral. I stayed in Alberta with my husband and children.

I was still clutching the letter in my hand when the door flew open as Brianna and R.J. returned home from school. I usually met them at the curb when they got off the bus, but I'd been lost in the past. I tucked the envelope in my back pocket and welcomed them.

"Hey guys! How was your day?"

"How come you didn't meet us at the bus?" R.J. asked.

"I guess I just lost track of time." I smiled and ran my fingers through his blond hair, identical to his father's.

"But you were right here at the door," Brianna pointed out.

I did not reply as my five and seven-year-olds looked at me, waiting for an explanation from a mommy who never broke routine.

"R.J., go set up the family room while I get the milk and cookies." Part of our routine was watching cartoons after school before they started their homework.

"Why isn't it ready?"

"I told you, silly. I lost track of time." I gave him a little push toward the living room and I turned toward the kitchen. Brianna followed me.

"What's that?" she said.

"What's what?" I pulled a jug of milk out of the refrigerator.

"In your back pocket."

"Oh, this," I pulled the envelope out and placed it on top of the fridge. "Just a bill."

She shrugged off her backpack and helped put glasses and a plate of homemade chocolate chip cookies on the tray.

After dinner. Ryan helped me bathe and put the children to bed before he went out. He worked as a junior accountant by day and studied to get his full degree at night.

"See you at ten-thirty," he said, kissing me on the cheek.

"Have fun," I said.

"Always do." He smiled, blew me another kiss and then left me alone in silence.

As I sipped my tea, I looked at the gallery of crayoned pictures on the fridge. My lips turned into a smile as I laid eyes on a photograph of our whole family taken at Ryan's parents' house last summer. Seeing his parents reminded me of my own and I looked up at the crumpled envelope on top of the fridge. I sighed, put my cup down and pushed away from the counter.

After retrieving the envelope, I flattened the wrinkled paper and slipped a finger beneath the flap. It opened easily. I pulled out a single sheet of paper and unfolded it. My father's handwriting lined the page.

"Dear Rachel, your mother has passed away. On her deathbed she made me promise to forgive you. Funny thing is I forgave you a long time ago, I was just too stubborn to admit it."

I stopped reading to wipe tears from my eyes. I took a sip of tea, wiped my eyes again, and read on.

"I have seen pictures of your beautiful children. I would like to come out and visit you and your family, if that's okay with you. I understand if you don't want to see me, but I am an old man, alone now and don't know how much time I have left. I want to make amends before it's too late."

I let the note paper fall to the counter, released a breath I hadn't realized I'd been holding and began to sob. If only I had gone to my mother's funeral. If only the letter hadn't gotten lost, then my father would have met my family and maybe we could have erased the painful years of silence. I could have felt his bear-hug of an embrace once more.

The more I bawled, the more my chest hurt. I took a deep breath and another sip of tea. I wiped at my eyes, surprised at the depth of the pain I was feeling. I looked at the family photo again. I'd never noticed before that Brianna and R.J. bore a strong resemblance to my father. Tears filled my eyes again. How could I not forgive him? My father may have been gone, but when I looked into my children's eyes, his love I had once known lived again.

"I try to leave out the parts that people skip."
~ Elmore Leonard

AM A BLUEBIRD
(Dedicated to my late father, John C. Bird)

I am a bluebird,
not only in name.
My spirit flies
with creative game.

Soaring and diving
I look for the words
to put to paper—
the weird, the absurd.

I call to my muse
from high in a tree
to bring inspiration
to the bluebird in me.

The song flows as
I chirp the verse –
a wellspring of rhyme
and the silence it bursts.

A bluebird I am
born from another
whose use of words
gave pleasure to others.

The death of one
brings another to be
carrying on a song
he sings through me.

March 29, 2008

UNKNOWING

I am lost in a cloud of unknowing
unaware of where life is going
What is it that
God is showing to me
that through the clouds I cannot see?
Happiness eludes me
as I travel this lonely road
I carry a heavy load within a heart
of thin skin that continues to beat
though I know not why

Just as the clouds in the sky
cover the sun
I cannot see where to run
to escape the doldrums of life
Though the sun rises each day
my face does not portray the joy
I should display
for the gift God has given me,
the gift of life and being free
to choose my own path
my destiny.

February 21, 2010

Shirley Bray

Shirley currently lives in Ontario, Canada where she designs and creates websites. She also edits and produces videos with a little audio editing thrown in.

In her spare time, she writes fantasy to satisfy a vivid imagination and is part of the Headwaters Writers' Guild. Shirley has written numerous short stories and several pieces of poetry. Currently, she is working on a fantasy novel, which is in the first draft of edits.

DEADLINE

Ted banged on the keys of his old Underwood typewriter. He hated computers; they always caused him grief. Last summer, he'd gotten so frustrated with the one he had, he threw it out of his cottage window. He regretted it after it landed in ten feet of water, but he wasn't about to fish it out.

He was on a tight deadline—if only he had started work on his manuscript the moment he had thought of the idea and presented it to his publisher. But that was not his style. He always left things to the last minute, creating excuse after excuse why he couldn't start. His favourite was he had to get the concept clear in his mind before he put anything down on paper. Now here he was, working day and night in his island cottage, unshaven and unwashed for the third straight day, working desperately to get his thoughts down on paper, shaping the criminal investigations of Detective Gerry Tellson before this afternoon's six o'clock deadline.

Piles of crumpled pieces of paper surrounded the wastebasket.

His aim was not good and right now he didn't care where the paper ended up. Opened cans of stew and soup adorned the countertop by the window, adding to the cottage clutter.

Only eight hours left, just enough time to get into town and get his work to his publisher, Oscar Woodhouse. Ted put the final touches to the manuscript, hit the carriage return, ripped the page out of the typewriter and unceremoniously stuffed the ten pages into a crumpled, tea-stained brown envelope.

Ted quickly showered and grabbed a wrinkled green shirt and a pair of ripped jeans from the laundry hamper. He pulled on the clothes as he headed towards the old wooden door that squeaked as he pulled on the latch. Launching himself from the threshold, he ran down the winding path, heading for the dock.

Living on an island had its advantages: no noisy neighbours, barking dogs, or uninvited sales agents. The disadvantage was the boat ride to the nearest town across the next neck of Haven Lake.

Ted climbed into his twelve-foot aluminium boat, manuscript in hand. He noticed the dark clouds rapidly approaching from the north as he untied the boat; he knew it would rain within the hour. He hesitated, looking again at the sky, and decided he wasn't going to take any chances. He climbed back out of the boat and ran back to the cottage to get his rain gear. Reaching behind the front door, Ted grabbed his bright yellow raincoat from the rusty old nail and pulled on the jacket and matching hat as he made his way back to the dock.

His heart sank as he gazed out over the water; the boat was six feet away from the dock, drifting with the current toward the mainland, his manuscript on the back seat. How could he have been so careless? Ted's throat constricted as a rush of adrenalin flooded his veins. The lake was looking rough as his boat rocked back and forth with the swelling waves, moving it farther and farther away from the dock. He felt he had no choice but to swim out to retrieve the boat with his precious manuscript. Days of hard work had gone into his manuscript and he wasn't about to let it drift away. As he started to take off his left running shoe, he remembered his friend Peter had given him a telescopic gaffing hook for Christmas.

Hastily, he retrieved the hook from the small wooden box he used to store the life jackets at the end of the dock. He quickly extended the hook to its full length. Carefully, he manoeuvred the hook back and forth in the water, trying to snag the trailing end of the mooring rope, which was thankfully still within reach. Minutes seemed like hours until Ted finally reached down, grabbed the rope out of the hook and pulled the boat back into the dock.

His trusty Honda ten-horsepower motor purred at top revs as Ted raced across the lake. He unwillingly slowed down as he pulled into the marina, but not before causing a sizeable wake, rocking the nearby boats and floating docks.

He jumped out of the boat with his manuscript grasped tightly in his hand. Weaving in and out of the glaring fishermen lining the walkway, he made his way to his black, beaten up rust bucket of a truck. He quickly glanced at his watch; he had made good time and was thankful for that as he yanked open the door. In one fluid motion, he slid into the driver's seat and threw his manuscript down beside him. *Three hours left, more than enough time,* he thought as he slipped the key into the ignition.

A bang on the window stopped him just as he was ready to thrust the truck into gear. *What now?* He rolled down the window and looked into the stern face of a tall, well-built police officer.

"Sir, I cannot allow you to drive this vehicle. Please step out." The officer stepped back from the door, waiting for Ted to get out of the truck.

"Why not? I'm in a hurry. What's wrong with it?" Ted got out of the truck.

The officer pointed toward the ground. "You have four flat tires; you cannot drive the vehicle in this condition."

Ted threw up his hands. "Great, that's all I need." He had barely finished his sentence when the clouds opened up and a deluge poured down. "I have to get into town. I have a deadline," Ted continued, pacing back and forth, waving his arms.

"I can give you a ride if you like. I have to go that way." The officer smiled when he saw the relief on Ted's face. "You'll have to sit in the back seat." The officer pointed at the cruiser as he turned away from Ted.

Together, they sped into town with Ted thanking his rescuer all the way. The officer let Ted out into the pouring rain just in front of a century-old house. The house had been well looked after; its gray shuttered windows and oak door accented the distinctive red brick of the two-storey building.

Ted bounded up the carpet-covered stairs to the second floor, his clothes dripping as he took a deep breath outside his publisher's small office. He could hear the rain beating against the windows as he opened the door to greet his friend.

"Hi Oscar! Here it is. Finally finished." Ted threw the manuscript down on the cluttered desk, his raincoat dripping all over the carpet.

"This is great, Ted, and I think it's a first for you." Oscar, an elderly man with a round face, beamed as he picked up the manuscript. He adjusted his black-rimmed glasses, then pulled the crumpled papers from the envelope.

"What do you mean?" Ted looked at him, puzzled.

"You're a day early. The deadline isn't until tomorrow."

Ted sighed and thought back on the events of the day. He suddenly felt very tired. He took a staggering step back, then slumped into the beige cloth armchair next to Oscar's oak desk

I'M RETIRED

The dark shadows of the predawn clouds parted as Wes glanced down at the clock in the dash of his minivan. Five o'clock! He had driven all night, his investigation finally finished to everyone's satisfaction. He was now officially retired, after a thirty-year career as a private investigator. He sighed. *A hot cup of coffee would hit the spot right about now*, he thought.

He rounded the bend for the Highway 9 off-ramp heading north toward the intersection at Highway 10 and Broadway. He had seen the black sedan in his rearview mirror, but hadn't paid too much attention to the fact that it was riding his rear bumper. He wasn't going to get annoyed—not now.

Wes signaled and cut across the northbound lanes of Highway 10 so he could get into the left-turn lane that would take him into downtown Orangeville.

He yawned, closing his eyes briefly. As he opened them again, the black sedan passed his blue minivan on the inside lane. It was obvious the driver was trying to beat him to the left-turn lane before the light turned red. The sedan cut in front of Wes, forcing him to slam on his brakes.

"What the . . . " Wes muttered a few choice words as he followed the sedan around the corner. In a way, he was glad the driver had forced him to slow down.

A car horn sounded, but Wes ignored it as he turned out of the intersection heading uptown. The second blare got his attention. He realized that his attention on the sedan had distracted him from the road. He had driven into the wrong lane.

He froze at the wheel, watching as a car swerved to avoid him. He quickly turned the wheel, avoiding a transport truck as it whooshed by, shaking his van in its wake.

"That's it," Wes mumbled under his breath. He headed towardsthe coffee shop just up the road. Still shaken, he parked his van outside the yellow lines.

Inside, he smiled at the pale-faced blonde behind the counter as he paid for an extra-large coffee. Choosing a window seat, he sat down and gazed out of the window. As he surveyed the parking lot, he noticed the black sedan parked near the entrance to the drive-through. Wes shook his head and ignored it.

The coffee smelled good as he lifted the cup and sipped. A burly, middle-aged man dressed in grubby overalls slammed his mug down on a nearby table. Wes frowned as he glanced in the man's direction, thinking there was no need for that type of display. Wes sat back in his chair, feeling the fatigue of all the driving seeping throughout his body. The thought of a comfortable bed loomed in his mind. He took another sip from his cup as he watched the start of the morning rush to work.

"You can't do that to her now," a husky voice rasped from behind him.

A younger male voice snarled back, "Why not? She deserves it and I'm looking forward to paying her back for what she did to me." His words dripped with hatred.

Wes sunk down in his chair hoping the two hadn't realized he had heard them.

"I can't wait to see her beg for her life," the man continued. "Do you know how long I've been planning this? Every item has been examined right down to the last detail. I've covered all the possible outcomes. Only you and I will know what really happened to her."

Wes shivered as the man let out a sinister laugh. He wanted to look behind him, but he knew if he did they would know he had been listening. Wes's investigative instincts tingled as he shifted his position.

"How will you do it and what type of stuff will you use?" the husky voice snapped.

Gripped with fear and panic, Wes's stomach turned over. He had to act, but how could he leave without drawing attention to himself? He had to notify the police, but what would he tell them? Would they even believe him? He needed more information. Wes decided the best thing to do was to get as much information as he could. His hand shook as he sipped his coffee, pretending to watch the cars coming and going from the parking lot. He was getting too old for this; besides, he was retired, he told himself . . . but he still listened.

"It's easy. I already have a quick-acting poison. It's one of those exotic concoctions—kills instantly on contact and it's undetectable by any known toxicology screening." The young man sounded proud.

The other voice emitted a raspy chuckle. "Remind me not to get on your bad side, Harry. I want to live a long time."

Wes caught the mention of the name. *At least it was something*, he thought.

Harry continued to explain his plan, adding how he would spread a thin film of the potion on a door handle. "It becomes inert after an hour and will leave no trace," he gloated. His voice echoed his pride in the plan. The husky voice whispered another name and a time.

Wes missed it. He gritted his teeth in frustration.

The door swung open, letting in a blast of cold air. Here was Wes's chance. He turned his head, straining to get a glimpse of the perpetrators behind him without them becoming aware of his actions. Alas, all he saw was the back of a head full of black, curly, shoulder-length hair—not enough to make an identification. The door slammed shut; a man made his way over to the table where the two men sat.

"Well, has the deed been done?" The voice sounded like it belonged to an elderly man.

Wes could hear the slight quiver of age as he spoke. There was a pause while the elderly man moved behind Wes. He felt him brush up against his chair.

Dare he look? He decided not to. He pulled in his chair and had another sip of coffee.

"Not yet. We've been waiting for the right time," the husky voice muttered.

"Today would be best." Harry's voice sounded stern, daring the other two to challenge his judgment.

The husky voice snarled, "We wanted to go over every item, in order, just to make sure we hadn't missed any details."

"That's good. It's the small details that will give you away," the elderly voice muttered.

Wes heard the chair legs scrape the floor as the old man sat down.

"Dress rehearsal is tonight. It will give you a chance to really live the characters."

Dress rehearsal? The words startled Wes; his heart almost stopped. Live the characters? The words swirled in his mind. What had he been listening to? He had been ready to run to the rescue of this mysterious woman and turn these men in for their murderous plan.

Wes stood up, turning to get a look at the actors. He walked out into the parking lot. The thought of trying to explain to the police struck him as funny. He snickered as he drove by the window, watching the threesome as he passed. He felt relieved that it was make-believe and he didn't have to be the knight in shining armour. Wes shook his head as he headed for home.

Three days later, Wes opened the morning paper. "Woman Murdered. No Suspects." The bold headline was sprawled across the front page. He dropped his cup, spilling hot coffee over the table. His heart pounded as he recalled the events in the coffee shop. He read on. The middle-aged woman had been an actress from the local theatre house. She had been found dead in her living room with no apparent reason for her demise. All of the tests had proven inconclusive.

Wes stared at the paper. Maybe they weren't rehearsing lines after all; maybe it had all been a ruse to mislead anyone who was listening to their conversation. He didn't know what to think. Wes cleaned up the spilled coffee, then paced back and forth, contemplating what he should do.

He ran through the overheard conversation in his mind. This was a murder plan if ever he had heard one. He had to make sure whether the three guys were actors rehearsing a play, or the cold-blooded murderers of the woman. Wes walked down the hallway of his bungalow.

He entered the bedroom and sighed as he made his way around the queen-size bed and opened the top drawer of the oak dresser. He reached into the right corner and pulled out a small silver key and an empty black shoulder holster. He threw the holster onto the bed.

He turned around and headed toward a small landscape painting with a hideous gold-painted frame hanging at the end of his bed. He pulled on the edge of the frame; it opened, revealing a hidden safe with a key slot. Wes slid the key into the slot, turned the key and pulled the handle to open the safe. He stood there for awhile before reaching in to retrieve a small revolver.

"No! I'm retired," he muttered out loud. He put the gun back into the safe, closed the door and slammed the painting frame back into place.

Wes walked to the head of his bed and reached for the phone on the side table. He dialed, then sat on the bed while he waited for the phone to connect.

"Can I speak to the detective in charge of the murder of the actress?" A wave of relief swept over him as he told the detective what he had overheard in the restaurant, giving a detailed description of the three men.

At least he could finally retire with a clear conscience . . . or could he?

"Substitute 'damn' every time you're inclined to write 'very;' your editor will delete it and the writing will be just as it should be."
~ Mark Twain

David Chesterton

David started life drawing at age 13 and created portraits of the Queen for local stores at the time of the Coronation. He did many portraits of senior officers in the R.A.F. For ten years, he was a member of the Head Hunters, a Newmarket group that met weekly to do portraiture. He has sketched and painted with many known artists, including A.J. Casson. After working in graphic design, he taught colour and creativity in community colleges for 25 years, and was a coordinator of Elderhosel travel programs. He has three self-published books: *My Caravan is a Rainbow, St Vincent Passage* and *Pigmented Spectacles,* and is a self-described "Jack of all trades, master of none."

LINE ASTERN
A true story. (Some names have been changed.)

The flight of Harvard training planes approached the airfield line astern. "Paddy," our Irish flight leader for the day, was in "Tail-end Charlie" position behind us, keeping us in a fairly straight line as we followed "Nobby" Clarke, our youngest pilot. He could concentrate on the runway and wasn't bumping around in the tropical thermals which we were fighting as we followed each other, our planes weaving in a slight crosswind. Southern Rhodesia was not the most comfortable place to land a plane just before noon. This line astern exercise needed far too much attention, and I had other things on my mind.

"Grampa Charles," my favourite grandfather, had died a week ago and I was three thousand miles away from Birstall, his village in England. The distance felt like a void between us and I was grieving my inability to say, "Goodbye."

"You're drifting to port number two." Paddy's brogue broke through my reverie and I juggled the stick to get back in line. Nobby was maintaining a good lead and was about a quarter of a mile from touchdown. Looking through my rearview mirror, I saw the others coming down behind me like three planes on an escalator. "Not too low, number one." Paddy came in again and I noticed that Nobby was —

"I'm losing power." Nobby's voice cut into my thoughts. His plane yawed. *This was a helluva place to lose power* I thought.

A voice from the control tower broke in. "Try giving it full throttle."

Nobby yelled, "It's totally dead, sir!"

The small line of thorny trees around the edge of the field thrust up toward us and Nobby tried to raise the nose of his aircraft to clear them. But that caused the plane to stall and we heard him wail, "Oh no." He tried to correct the stall, but the plane went into a steep dive toward the trees.

I watched, aghast. There was nothing I could do. I just wanted to give Nobby a chance to recover. I tried to slow time down. A bushman shaman had taught me that trick, but I needed to be calm and Nobby was too close to the ground.

When the plane hit, it exploded in a gouting ball of fire.

My mind went blank, and an eon later, I heard the voice of the control tower officer screaming into my headphones. I was flying straight and level about ten feet above the runway but at the far end, one thousand yards beyond the crash. "Full throttle, two-five-two! Full throttle. Go round again."

I thrust the throttle in and my engine's nose rose with a blaring roar of sound. *Why couldn't Nobby's engine do that?* It was an angry and pointless thought. I pulled back the stick and began a careful circuit. When I was half-way into the downwind leg it hit me. I'd have to fly right over the spot where Nobby's plane was burning furiously among the blazing tinder-dry trees. A fire tender was roaring down toward the spot, but I could see that Nobby had already been cremated.

My grandfather had wanted to be cremated, but my grandmother felt it was against her religion. I forced my mind away from that and began the crosswind leg. A glance around showed the others coming in a ragged line on the downwind leg.

A few moments later, I turned toward the runway and clouds of black smoke, rising from the fire. The fire crew was directing a steady stream of water into the heart of the blaze, but it didn't seem to be doing anything.

I came in a little higher than usual to fly over the worst of the smoke, but the control tower voice came through again.

"Normal approach, two-five-two, nose down." And, as I dutifully pointed the nose directly into the smoke plume, he said, "You're doing fine—you'll get through the smoke in a second. Two-seven-one you're a little close behind two-one-nine." His voice was calm and encouraging, and I felt more at ease.

I broke through the smoke, made a minor adjustment and lined up on the runway. In a few seconds I would be down and could rush back to the fire. I just felt I had to be near Nobby. A thermal lifted me and dropped me and I was about to touch down when the voice broke through again.

"Full throttle, two-five-two. Go round again." I couldn't believe his order. My wheels were almost touching the runway, but he yelled, "Full throttle, two-five-two. I repeat, go round again! That's an order!"

The voice was no longer calm and encouraging, but I had been trained well and again climbed up and into a second circuit.

Seething, I made my way around the airfield, hearing his similar "orders" to my flight companions and watching as they began their second circuit. With each successive, autocratic command my dislike for that voice increased. Again, I headed toward the smoke. Thinking my earlier, faulty approach might have been the reason why I had to go around again, I made a textbook approach and was about to touch down when that voice cut in for the third time.

"Full throttle, two-five-two. Go round again." This time he didn't even shout. He just exercised his damned authority. Choking down a desire to yell at him, I went around again.

On the fourth circuit, the fire truck had succeeded in quelling the fire, but that meant the skeleton of Nobby's plane was in clear view as I flew over. I couldn't resist a glance down at the cockpit. An ugly, charred figure sat in the burned-out wreck. As my wheels began to touch down, I realized what I had really known when I saw that fireball. It had been obvious, but my anger at the officer in the control tower had taken over any rational thought. Nobby was gone.

I just wanted to be with my friends on the ground so we could be together.

"Full throttle, two-five-two. Go round again." My anger became a coagulating mass of gall in my stomach. But I submissively went around again. My fuel was getting low and a few seconds later Paddy, also ordered into his fifth circuit, quietly reported, "Climbing as ordered, sir, but my flight are all getting low on fuel, sir."

"Noted, flight leader," was the terse response. My cold feeling of intense disgust of the man descended to icy hatred. Does the bastard want us all to crash? Overwrought, I knew as soon as we landed, I was going up to the control tower to punch that guy right in the nose. Assaulting an officer was a court-martial offence, but I didn't care. In fact, I felt a glow of excitement as I saw myself giving him a belt he'd never forget.

Paddy's voice, quiet and calm, broke into my fantasy. "As we fly over Nobby, let's wag our wings to him." And, for a moment, I forgot my seething hatred of the flight controller. I silently blessed Paddy. He had known we all wanted to do something after this feeling of helplessness.

"Do you want to go first, Paddy?"

"No, David. We'll stick to our flight order. Okay, number three, get back in line behind David, let's do this right . . . " We heard his intake of breath and then a soft, "For Nobby."

I thought about Nobby and my grandfather as I approached the wreckage and wagged my wings. Neither of them would have wanted me to do anything formal.

The wind seemed to cooperate with our salute to them. The final landing was a perfect line astern touch down.

We taxied to the parking zone where our course commander was waiting for us. Just as I knew he would do—not like that unthinking isolate in the control tower who was about to get ploughed.

I waited till we were all lined up and then cut my engine—the dial recorded empty. Bill Dawes, the ground crew leader for our flight, jammed the chocks under my wheels and came around behind the wing to watch me clamber out of the cockpit and jump to the ground.

"Sorry about Nobby, sir," he said. His eyes were red.

I put my hand around his shoulders. "Thanks Bill, we'll miss him in the Mess."

In a moment, my three flight buddies and I were beginning to swelter in our flight clothing but we hugged each other. The first time I'd ever done that to any of them. It gave me a feeling of warmth for them I'd never been able to express. And my tension began to drain away.

Our course commander, Flight Lieutenant Ron Morgan, joined us and, in typical British style, shook hands all around—but he made eye contact with each one of us. I had always liked his eyes, generally smiling or observing everything. But when it was my turn, there was a feeling of someone looking right into me, sharing.

He led us to the de-briefing room and gave us a moment to get out of our cumbersome flight clothing. As I dropped my flight jacket and helmet onto one of the chairs, I was trying to figure out how to get out of there and up to that control tower.

"Right now, I imagine all of you are torn between two emotions." Morgan's voice broke into my thoughts as we sat down in front of him. "You want to get out there and pay your respects to Nobby, but I'm betting you also want to get up to the control tower and either punch Flight Lieutenant Kingsley in the eye, or at least ream him out."

We stared at him for a moment, looked at each other, and then we started to chuckle. In the two years we had been together, we thought we knew each other and our commander, but this was another shared experience that helped release the tension.

"I'm here to dissuade you from doing both." He paused and looked at each one us. "There is absolutely nothing you can do for Nobby now . . . and I feel he would want you to remember him as he was when you sat here for this morning's flight plans."

"As for the desire to punch up Flight-Lieutenant Kingsley, I'd rather you didn't as I'd hate to sit in on your court martials." He grinned, but then looked out the window for a second. "You've just been through an experience which will make you better pilots. If Kingsley hadn't done what he did to you, one or more of you would never fly again. Those repeated touch and gos made you furious with him. And that anger replaced your initial fears and horror at Nobby's appalling death."

"But he didn't care, sir," I argued. "His voice was absolutely dead."

Morgan paused for a moment, but his eyes never left mine. "It's bound to come out later, so I may as well tell you now. Flight Lieutenant Kingsley did exactly what he is trained to do, despite the fact he was also suffering a terrible crisis of his own." He turned to look out the window and we followed his gaze. A haze of smoke hung in the air. His voice was quiet and gruff as he said, "Nobby's mother is Kingsley's sister."

"There's nothing to writing.
All you do is sit down at a typewriter
and open a vein."
~Walter Wellesley "Red" Smith

j.m.crole

Jenn has enjoyed writing poetry and journaling for the last 23 years. Her early works were inspired by the awkward life of a broken hearted teenager; she continues to write on self discovery, love and other complications. She currently lives in Orangeville, with her dog, Justine, just around the corner from her niece and nephew.

ETERNAL ROSE

Gracefully she picked up the flower,
a pretty shade of rose,
and took a deep breath in her nose.
The sweet scent travelled through her body,
leaving her dizzy and feeling oddly.
"This flower is for you," she said,
"I shall place it on your eternal bed.
Then you will know I was here.
To give you my love and shed a tear."

SPARKLING

A gem sparkling,
value,
meaning to exist.
Failure to complete.
Fog . . . a mist that guides,
darkness bleeds, the nothingness of why.
Ever present, past belonging . . .
velvet, smooth, tasty . . .
a regret, more wise.
Falling clouds, leave behind a trail,
to one day return.
Sunny, joyful, loved,
time heals,
hollow heart,
forgives the rest.
A place to stand,
strength to fall . . .
message summoned from a dream.
Sparkling memories,
and all that's in between.

SUPERSTITION

A distant whispering, bellowing in the darkness,
changing directions is never an easy task.
Dawning a new beginning, afraid to fall,
unthawing the emotions left underneath it all.
Infected by pain and the unwillingness to resist,
staying still so long you cease to exist.
Budding flowers starving for nutrition,
hungry for sunlight and a little superstition.
A magic melody clouds the sky,
passionate words keep my memory high.
Travelling the night to fall back in,
a peak of heaven, away from sin.
Feet flat on the ground, eyes to the sky . . . feeling
something profound and the need to ask why.

Ruth Cunningham

Ruth is a seeker, a listener and a visionary. She was born in Kelowna, B.C. and has worked and lived in B.C., Alberta, Saskatchewan, Ontario and Washington State. She now resides in the Ontario countryside between Cambridge and Guelph, with her husband, George, and until recently their 21-year-old cat, Min who is now frolicking on the other side. Her personal life story is bound by her work with the Speaker Material and its self-to-Self life study. To read more about Ruth and her work, go to www.self-to-self.com

INSPIRATION

What is inspiration—and where does it come from? A dictionary definition helps us with a factual common meaning, and religion supplies us *its* particular view of inspiration's source. Yet as a personal understanding, inspiration defies dogmatic tags and motives, as each of us defines it from our own experience and seeks its creative essence through our own intuitive rootage.

Whether it graces a Monet canvas, waltzes through a Mozart melody, leaps triumphantly as the "Eureka!" of a sublime insight or revolutionary discovery, whether it rhymes within a mystically metered quatrain, or surges within a symphonic crescendo, inspiration enriches both the creator and created. Arousing, affecting, animating, astonishing, exhilarating, encouraging, stimulating and stirring— inspiration always elicits an unforgettable thrill. With its emotive eloquence equally illuminating listener and speaker, inspiration eternally defies our complete capture.

As a poet, I have a history with inspiration, and a future fashioned from each day's regard for this vital, vaporous value that I strive to infuse into my words. Yet, every genre of creativity invokes its own mysterious muse and incorporates inspiration's magical immanence. While *you* might look to Hestia, the Greek Goddess of Architecture for your divine designs, I might look to Brigit, the Celtic Writer's Goddess of Inspiration, Poetry and Prose to ignite my creative spark.

Perhaps the illusive nature and source of inspiration escapes our everyday apprehension, and maybe we cannot always articulate our inward grasp or logically reason our explanation of it. However, each of us recognizes the enchanted joy of the truly inspired when we find it—and are gladly grateful for this gracious gift of the Goddess.

> *"The difference between the right word*
> *and the almost right word*
> *is the difference between*
> *lightning and a lightning bug."*
> *~ Mark Twain*

INSPIRATION

climb

Somewhere in the Deep Divine   mountains

clouds   and

descend

as Inspiration takes to wing
to join the joy of newborn spring
upon her wake of dreams I fly
as if life's fetters to defy

The rapturous route of living's stream
through chiseled space-and-time
unseen
in tumbling tumult
falls away
beneath the weight
of every day
for I—like all
remain enslaved
by dusk and dawn
from birth to grave

Yet, somewhere in the deep divine
when truth ascends
the stars align
as Inspiration spreads her wings
I chase the glint
of unnamed things
and speed upon her slipstream's trail
to slide behind her mystery's veil

and seek to find
in my own heart
her magic awe
at each day's start

Should Inspiration know my name
and call to me
beyond life's frame
of somber scenes
and vapid views
beyond my mindscape's
mundane hues
that I might find within her call
each season's secret to enthrall
and know life's grander course redeemed
in every new day's dawn
re-dreamed.

"Fill your paper with the breathings
of your heart."
~ William Wordsworth

WORDS

As an elemental component of language, words are the key carriers of meaning that variously and vibrantly voice our individuation into our individuality. Words are our conceptual organizers—the interpreters of our ideas, the translators of our thinking, the expressers of our experiences and the bastions of our beliefs. Through our words, we can share our sense, invoke our intent, verify our views, and thus render our interpretations of the intangible world of the mental into the concretized world of the corporeal as manifest communication.

Words reflect the creative essence of humanhood and prescribe our earth-hood and spirit-hood as the mind-to-matter marriage that speaks our identity to reverberate from the inside out. From the mundane to the mythic, the pedestrian to the prophetic, the microcosmic to the macrocosmic, words wield a wondrous power to transcribe, transpose and transport—record, rearrange and reveal. Words, strung together into life's living language, express more than their singular definitions; they conjure, clarify and convey the infinite nuances that name our very nature.

I've talked to many writers who feel as I do as a poet, as I consider words the lifeblood of my craft. As the line from one my poems about writing poetry explains, often "I cannot tell where I end and you begin."

WORDS

Today
I am made up
  of words

Literacy's landmarks—
 rubble and rabble
mythic as memory—
  the ruins of Babble
a heart-hunted history—
   mind-sprouted things
from the chrysalis to Time
   before it grew wings

I am verbiage flying
set on a course
  of exploiting
       itinerant adjectives—vagrant vowels
that betray no remorse
  as they maim with their scorn
       and murderous scowls
they retreat
  but remain
unaware of themselves
as anything less
   than the haunt of our howls;

No need to remember
they ever were more
once rhymed-up with reason
   forgotten before
this particular page
     pleaded until
          it was filled
              with the will
of these words
   keeping score
too big—too loud
to hide in the crowded
   cocoon of my mind
they spit and they spatter—
flow till they flood
over my senses they rain
with a sudden
          reckless refrain
to land with a thud
          on the innocent brain

Then queerly content
they are energy spent
expensive as tears
unreturnable gifts
   packaged in pain
tied up in the tatters
of hopes and fears
          the cost of our years
that can't come again

Today
I am made up
  of words

Like concrete creatures
  awakened too soon
from their soft earth dream
  under yellow moon
no need to remember
  what yesterday means
content with their truths
  their reality seems
    monolithic as mammoths
right till the instant
  they all disappear
and all that is left
  is no one
    to hear
that today
  I am made up
of words

J. C. Dumas

J.C. is a founding member of the Headwaters Writers' Guild. He always told stories but being dyslexic, he believed it would be impossible for him to become a writer. A year and a half after a serious accident, he started to write. In March 2003, he joined the late Ed Wildman's writing workshops. Ed's encouragement inspired J.C. to write poetry. His poem, *My Guardian Angel,* is published in the *The New Top Ten Joy Journal.*

He lives with his wife, two daughters, a granddaughter, and numerous pets.

GUARDIAN ANGEL

She travels faster than the speed of light.
She travels with me day and night.
She is gentle, touching my inner soul.
She reminds me of all my goals.
She follows me when I'm awake.
She licks her lips when I eat cake.
She huddles by my side night and day.
She never asks if she can stay.
She hugs me close when I cry.
She wipes the last tears from my eye.
She helped my mother during my birth.
She gave thanks that I had arrived here on earth.
She will always be a close friend.

She will protect me when I reach my last bend.
She will take me back home when I die.
Together we will fly through God's blue sky.

MICHELLE

The first time I saw you, I started to cry
Tears of joy rolled down from my eyes
My hand reached out to touch your face
The angels had filled your heart with grace

You are the sun that brings the perfect light
You are the moon that brightens the night
You are the child who has conquered her dreams
You are the woman who reigns supreme

Your gentle hugs created the greatest moments in time
I could almost hear the church bells chime
Today, I walked you down the aisle
It caused my heart to leap a mile

Every moment of my life, I knew
I couldn't ever imagine my world without you
I am proud of you, my first child
For you, I'd walk a thousand miles

SAVE ME

Save me from
My emptiness
My worthlessness
My shadows
My highs and lows
My guilt
My filth
My frustrations
My delusions
My sorrows
My tomorrows
My hate
My fate
My fears
My tears
My addictions
My frictions
My abuse
My short fuse
My shame
My pain
My belligerence
Be my deliverance
Save me from myself
And my closed doors
Help me change and nothing more

The writer of the following story requested to be anonymous.

HAYWIRE – The Absence Of Laughter

The too-thin cat stared at the world from the apartment window giving the illusion of order. The remnants of torn materials of yellow and green were held together by the smashed cardboard that covered the windows. A symbol of the smashed lives that nightly entered, got the high of the needle and left in the darkness. The broken windows bearing mute testimony of the foot traffic.

"Don't let the needle mark show on my arm," the young teen remarked. I heard her feet hit the floor as she entered the apartment. Minutes later, she left to be replaced by one of the next dozen or so. Money flowed, the noise escalated.

"Is he dead?"

"Don't even say that," the hushed voice of the dealer responded. Sure enough, the earlier squeal followed by kicking of the boots against the wall was replaced by Joe's incoherent noises as the drug's reaction increased.

Screaming hysterically at five in the morning, the stringy haired young woman with the broken and battered shoes left by the door. Her use was accomplished. She was told earlier in the night, "get your top off."

The two older cops were not duped. Their hands were tied for lack of a warrant to search the premises and they had no choice but leave.

"Did you ever see so many people crowded into one spot? Not a stick of furniture upright. There's a bunch of kids that missed the lesson on say no to drugs. Let's go get a coffee."

The dealer kept a sharp eye. Joe was screeching at the top of his lungs. He reached for the phone and called his bud to come pick him up. The truck pulled into the driveway as three husky lads escorted Joe into the passenger side.

"The cops are after me about selling to this one dude. He shot up in a hotel room in town and lost his f****** mind. Truthfully, it may have been my drugs or not. How the hell would I remember?" The twenty something young man hung his head.

His drug boss passed him the joint. "Just keep pleading your innocence and let it pass, Son. Playing the drug game comes with a price, is all."

"I hate only certain aspects of jail. Mostly, I don't give a damn or give it a thought."

The door is broken, the sign says children at play. The understatement of the year is taped into place in a way that tells the dealer if entry has been made during his absence.

Furniture, a headboard with a clear shape of the boot that smashed it into pieces, a chair with a severed leg, a table torn in half was among the rubble that made it to the garbage.Less portable damage came in the form of a splintered fire door, a huge pane of glass that once graced the entrance to the building and the small panes in a once fine cupboard booted into oblivion. The glass at the side door met with the same fate. The steel piece that covered the lock on the side door was jimmied the night the card was taken to all the locks in the lower level.

Tommy lay outside her door at six in the evening.   The neighbour stemmed the blood that flowed from his face, cleaned him up after he screamed for help. Four sturdy enforcers pounded his face to pulp. A brave woman in her own right, Mary stepped into the corridor.

She returned for a wet facecloth, cleaned him up following the fast demise of the four cowards. Profuse thanks followed. Tom left never to return.

Surf's up.   The text message alerted young users from twenty miles away.   Thursday during the supper hour the young people began the invasion.   They pounded on corridor walls, shouted to each other, knocked down pictures from the walls and generally created chaos in their wake. All a prelude to the drug sales that would follow the local bar scene.

The core group stepped inside apartment 4. The music was noisy and upbeat.   Later, the one drum monotonous drug music would play the night away. Neighbours woke to the din. He looked out to survey the scene from his darkened apartment.   The holiday week-end escalated into a drug fest.

Crowds of young men and women stood in the street, on the steps and on the seedy unkept lawn. Each awaited his or her turn for the drug of choice.   Once administered, paid and the next group were allowed to gain access by the darkened front window. If the neighbours didn't sleep, so what.

Doors slammed, the hysteria mounted. Tired and frustrated neighbours finally summoned the police. Five cruisers gathered but once again as they searched for drug paraphernalia and awaited a search warrant, they were denied access to the apartment.

An artificial hush fell as the crowd dispersed. The dealing resumed within an hour of the police departure. Weary residents awaited the five A.M. hour. This time the hysterical young woman remained to witness the usual early morning battle between the two brothers, one the dealer and the other the addict.

A frustrated apartment dweller pounded on her living room window as a young man walked within a foot of it in the dark.

"Get away."

He looked back over his shoulder and prepared a get-away, running into the lawn furniture. She laughed. Suddenly, she realized the key.

There it was. Laughter. The absence of laughter meant drugs were being administered and sold. The presence of laughter was a sign of no drugs and a more wholesome party style. Perhaps just Ecstasy and it was a foregone that no drugs meant less obnoxious behavior.

The time changed earlier this year. With it came the usual Saturday night commotions. Finally, he drifted off to sleep for a few minutes. Suddenly, the ear-splitting noise of crashing glass. He ran to the window for a look. Ice slicked over the street. Had a car careened into the building?

Later, the glass was visible with the return of a cold gray dawn. Property management came sometime during that Sunday. They cleaned up except for the numerous shards of glass that remained from the last event.

Good news. Property management reported months back that although it is hard to evict these days, the culprits will be leaving unit 4. The dealing gradually ceased. Broken furniture graced the curb. The lawn boasts timothy spikes two feet high.

Suddenly, he hears the lawn mower. It cuts down the spikes and all else in its path. He is reminded that this is synonymous of the young lives that are being cut down with the use of drugs. Families who expect their children to carry on in their wake; their legacy and reason for having lived are sorely disappointed. Hope is destroyed much like the timothy. He bows his head and weeps.

> *"The best style is the style you don't notice".*
> *~Somerset Maugham*

Ashley Haworth

Ashley is a small town girl with the goal of becoming a published author. She loves poetry, long walks on the beach and poking dead things with a stick. She spends much of her time thinking about human nature, especially the human's abject fascination with things that scare them. She writes short horror stories and is currently working on her first novel. She hopes the final product will make society "wake up" and realize what is happening to the world and how all the good things in life can disappear in a moment.

Ashley also writes poems that mostly concern specific emotions or personalities. However, she is working to expand her horizons in every regard to writing.

IDENTITY

Let night and day be enemies,
Fighting for position in the sky,
In a never-ending battle
Of blinding light and shrouding dark.

I am the sunset and sunrise
The in-between of sides.
Back and forth I go,
Neither choosing, nor preferring.

Why choose to be so bright,
Yet only be so dark
From morn' to night?

Why choose to be so dark,
While wishing for the light
As the moon is burning bright?

I'd rather be a fleeting moment
Of vibrant and vapid colors,
As cools and warms flash
Across the sky.

I can be a mixture of reds,
With a sea of blue;
Tiny streaks of purple
Or dotted with shades of yellow hue.

Why choose to be one color
Always seen, always granted,
Each and every day?

Why choose to be of none
Only to be treated as a void
Each and every night?

Let night be dark and void
The day bright and granted.
I will take my moment,
Which is captured for a lifetime
With the sunrises of the past,
And the sunsets that will last.

TRANQUILITY

My eyes are aflutter,
Meeting soft, reflected light,
As I hear the mutter
Of water's descending flight.

I stand in shallow water pools;
Waves moving to and fro.
The centre shines with infinite jewels
That cast the faintest glow.

I don't feel so cold,
Even with icy tones
Sparkling on the green gold
Of moss on stones.

I breathe out a long sigh—
Wispy wind washes over me
As I look to the sky
To see the starry sea.

Just above the central sight,
A floating harp plays
And music fills the night
Drawing my softest gaze.

The melody follows a rhythmic tune,
Of waterfalls making the walls,
Of chambers open to the moon,
And echoes its liquid calls.

My eyes close once more
And I wander blindly
Towards the music to explore
The song playing kindly.

There's sudden light upon the pools;
The day comes so soon,
Forgetting a night's brightly shining jewels,
Forgetting the slowly fading tune …

*"Ink on paper is as beautiful to me
as flowers on the mountains;
God composes, why shouldn't we?"
~ Terri Guillemets*

Marilyn Kleiber

Marilyn has been writing (and dating) for years.   Early on in both endeavours, she found that having a rather warped sense of humour was exactly what she needed to get through the challenges and emerge laughing, thus she's enjoyed the entire journey. Marilyn's vow to have no regrets when it comes time to shuffle off this "mortal coil," has prompted her to sample a large variety of careers and sports—everything from radio management to scuba diving, sailing and climbing tall trees.

THE BLIND DATE

"I don't know why I ever signed up for this crazy dating service!"

"Of course you do, Sherry," Jackie said.   "You've suddenly become single again, you're a total loss at getting dates on your own and you're hanging around your apartment dressed in your old tatty robe eating Häagen-Dazs by the gallon.   Girlfriend, you need to get out."

Sherry sighed. "I know all that, but you should've seen the two guys they've sent as blind dates so far."

"Ugh?"

"Major Ugh! The first was seventeen years older than me, but he seemed okay when I spoke to him. It was when we met for dinner that he showed his true colours.   He spent most of the time moaning about his 'money-grabbing, gold-digging' ex-wife. And when dessert came, he reached for his heart pills."

"OMG!"

"Yeah, there I am, sitting in this restaurant, having a vision of us on our wedding day. As the minister says, 'I now pronounce you man and wife,' my new husband croaks and, out of nowhere, his ex-wife runs in, waving a lawsuit at me over the estate."

Jackie chuckled. "So what about date number two?"

"Well, at first I was interested when he told me was French-Canadian. I love how romantic the French are. But he had been living in the U.S. for twelve years, so I had no idea how much French charm he still had."

She paused. "When he called to arrange our meet, I was a little nervous when he told me I would recognize him by his snakeskin cowboy boots."

"Snakeskin? Oh that's too funny. I get it you're not into cowboy boots?"

"You know I can't stand country and western music and all that stuff, and somehow I didn't think he'd turn out to be a 'Mr. Greenpeace.'"

"So, how did it go?"

"Not good. From the very beginning he grumped about Canadians and the Canadian government for not allowing him to bring his guns across the boarder . . . which, I might add, he kept in his glove compartment."

"Guns? Wow, he is a cowboy."

"Then he began complaining about restaurant prices and the selections we have here. We were in a simple family restaurant. You know the kind—standard menu and reasonable prices. Guess he prefers rattlesnake or prairie dog cooked over an open fire, for only the cost of a bullet or two!"

Jackie shook her head. "Only you could get involved in something so weird. So, what did you do?"

"I just wanted to escape, so I told him I had forgotten to take out my clothes from the machines at the laundromat, and I ran for my car. Come to think of it, I don't think he had me pegged as the love of his life either. Probably didn't like the way I called him gun-crazy."

"Sherry, you either have to keep your options and your attitude open, or don't accept any more blind dates from Dates-R-Us."

"Jackie, this cost me over a thousand dollars. I hate waste and I want my money's worth."

Jackie rolled her eyes. "So how many more dates with jerks do you consider will be getting your money's worth?"

Sherry laughed. "You're right. Sometimes it is better to cut your losses, but I do have one more date scheduled tonight, and this one sounds promising."

"In what way?"

"Well, his profile stated that he's a successful in-house salesman with Brigg Manufacturing, and he signed up for introductions because he's recently been transferred here from Ohio. He's my age, also divorced, no kids and loves music. He sounded nice on the phone."

"Hey, call me when you get home," Jackie said. "I want to know all the details . . . the good, the bad aaaand the ugly."

"Okay, I will. Well, I gotta run, thanks for the lunch and for the sympathetic ear."

9:45 that same night.

"Hi Jackie—I just got home."

"Hold it a minute, I just have to turn down the radio." The phone clunked on the table. "Okay, give me the juice."

"I was surprised at how good looking he was, and his bod was A-1 buff. I met him at Le Cercle, and he was sitting at the table with wine and a bunch of daisies for me."

"Wow, Le Cercle is really expensive. Sounds like you got a good one this time, girl."

"Well, yeah, money seemed to be no problem, and the wine was incredible."

"Hey, kiddo, why do I think I'm hearing a 'but' in your voice?"

"There's more than one—too many, as a matter of fact. He doesn't share my love of art and he never will, and he has no interest in photography. Plus, he thinks he wouldn't make a good father, so kids are probably out."

"And there's your clock, ticking away," Jackie said.

"I know! I know, and I don't think there's room for negotiation, 'cause he is so rigid about what he wants and doesn't want. He's not what you'd call a flexible guy. I can't imagine him doing anything really spontaneous. However, the biggest rock in the road is that he has no sense of humour. None! Nada! Nein!"

"Sherry—I think it is time you cut and run on this one."

"You're right. This is absolutely the last date I will accept from Dates-R-Us."

"Good. Time to move on, hon."

"Jackie, you can stop drilling, you've struck oil. Oh, by the way there was something really rather odd about the date. Quite bizarre actually."

"What was that?"

"When I sat down, I noticed a white cane beside his chair. He really was a blind date!"

DREAM LOVER

Like a great cat he moves
long and lithe
silently
on great furred and padded paws
no wasted motion.
I watch.
Muscles bunch and ripple
satin over steel.
Midnight eyes pin me to place
and probe beneath my soul.
I am mesmerized.
Stillness surrounds him.
I turn away seeking control
Silence.
When I look back
nothing but smoke remains.
Relief.
It was but fantasy and
I am released
but disappointed.
Then on my neck hot cinnamon breath
velvet touches on my body.
Fever!
Surrender!

WHAT IS FAITH?

"Faith! What is faith?" Debbie waved her arms about in frustration.

"Faith is that absolute belief in the unfolding of certain events to an expected conclusion," John said.

"Okay, that's the textbook answer, but the real question is, how do we know that faith is justified? What proof is there?"

John squinted at the ceiling, thinking. "Well, when the events really do come about, I guess. When the events or things actually manifest."

"John, that doesn't really tell me anything. For example, if someone has faith that they will go to heaven when they die, how will we know that their faith was warranted?"

"Well, since they are no longer around in their physical bodies, and since it is their faith we are discussing and they have not come back to tell us their faith was misplaced, we have to assume they did indeed end up in heaven."

"Oh, no you don't! Assumptions do not qualify as proof." She prodded him in the chest.

"Hey, Deb, be careful, I bruise easily."

"Don't be silly, John. You need to be able to prove that faith is deserved."

John sighed. "Deb, you're like a dog with a bone. Let's make it simple. When you buy butter, where do you go?"

"To the grocery store, of course."

"Why?"

"Because, duh, that's where butter is sold."

John grinned at her triumphantly. "I rest my case"

Deb scowled at him. "What do you mean you 'rest your case?'"

"You have faith that grocery stores carry butter!"

Ron Lehman

Ron was born at home in 1931 in Long Branch, ON. He worked in the electrical trade from 1952 to 2007 with stops in sales and Real Estate. Lovingly helped raise three daughters and a son, and in 1970 took up hobby farming in Mono Twp. where he designed and constructed a large addition to the family home. He earned his pilot's license in 1957, volunteered with Big Brothers Association as a Big Brother and Board Executive in the '60's, and in 1989 won the Top Hat Award for service to Toronto's oldest sailing establishment.

He was an avid skier on the Ontario Track 3 Ski Association, instructor of disabled children for six years, and served on his church Parish Council for two years. Growing up during WWII and serving in the Navy in the '50's provided Ron with valuable material for the following story.

TEARS FOR OUR FALLEN

Brettville sur Laize, Commnwealth Graves Cemetery

It was a beautiful June Spring day in Normandy 2004. A gentle breeze brought pleasant odors of wheat fields and wild flowers across an almost cloudless sky. If you closed your eyes and let your senses take in nature, you might think you were in Southern Ontario, and not in France. We observed a traditional silence as we traced a path through the headstones of fallen soldiers honouring the fallen comrades of seventeen members of our tour group by placing the

Regimental flag of The Queen's Own Rifles on their graves. My part was to follow the 'Honour Guard' and place a small amount of Canadian soil on their graves—soil which had been blessed by my Parish priest.

These men had lost their battle for life in early August, 1944 during the Allied push from Caen to Falaise in the code named "Totalize" battle, mainly a very large force of tanks and supporting infantry to speed up a stalled campaign. The fighting was fiercely hot that sweltering August, and the upper echelon of command could sense that a victory here may shorten WWII in Europe, which meant the stakes were high and defeat was not a part of the battle plan.

We completed our solemn walk and the colour party began to leave the cemetery for the bus to return to our hotel.

I purposely lagged behind to take a last look over the many headstones and at the beauty of the landscape in and around this hallowed place. As I walked slowly, I caught a glimpse of someone laying on a grave some five rows to my left. Stopping for a better view, I recognized it was a veteran who was by now kneeling before the headstone with his head bowed low. My first instinct was to leave him with his grief, but a strong voice inside prompted a meeting with this old warrior.

I retraced my steps to the row where he was and slowly walked to his side. He was sobbing and talking to the man in the grave.

As he became aware of my presence, I knelt beside him and put my right arm about his slouched shoulders. We held a long silence until I asked, "Is this your friend?"

"Yes, my very best friend. We grew up together, joined the North Nova Scotia Highlanders just after the war started and fought together until Jock was killed." He sobbed as we talked and tears flowed down my cheeks as well.

Leaning against the grave marker was an old photograph in which there were two soldiers and two ladies, one a bride and the other a bridesmaid, so I asked him if it was him and his friend. He replied, "Yes, this was taken three weeks before we shipped out, it was Jock's wedding day and I was his best man."

With those words he showed me the picture and I took the opportunity to embrace him. We were almost lying on Jock's grave with the veteran's head on my shoulder and his tears wetting my Naval jacket. Time stood still as I tried to fathom the depth of his sorrow. He said, "It has taken me sixty years to come back here and say goodbye to him."

I imagined the bonds between these men was so strong that saying a final goodbye was an almost insurmountable obstacle, but the passage of many years and old age gave him a sense of duty to say his goodbye.

The thought of perhaps easing his pain with an offer of some Canadian-blessed soil came to mind so I asked him if he would like to have some to sprinkle on his friend's grave. I removed the container of sand from my pocket and poured some into his cupped hand. We said a prayer together over the soil and he reverently sprinkled it among the flowers in front of the headstone. He said, "There Jock you are now back in Canada with us."

We stood up and embraced. "That was the nicest thing anyone has done for me," he said. "You have made it all worthwhile, coming over to say my last farewell to my friend. Thank you."

We shook hands, saluted each other and I took my leave back to the bus.

Plouescat, on the Northern Coast of Brittany.

Let's skip the clock ahead to Brittany, May 2005, from Normandy 2004, and a damp misty day in this small town on the west arm of the English Channel, a rugged coastline of rock and small islands where many ships have foundered down through the ages. Not an area suited to modern fighting ships to pursue each other in the dark of night.

My family and I were here to visit the local cemetery where fifty one Canadians are buried, following a fierce naval battle.

On the night of April 29, 1944 four destroyer class ships—two German and two Canadian—engaged in a momentous sea battle. The Canadian ship Athabaskan* was a victim of a torpedo and she sank in minutes. Those not killed in the initial action found themselves in the cold water waiting rescue. Some were picked up by the remaining Canadian destroyer HMCS Haida, others later, by the German Naval rescue service. The remainder were left to their own survival in the icy water.

Fifty-one had died in the cold night, their bodies left to wash up on a hostile shore.

Plouescat is a pretty town with friendly inhabitants and our stay in a local Bed and Breakfast on the edge of town was memorable. At breakfast we huddled around the kitchen table discussing this famous ship, as our hosts brought out several books about it—some in English, but most in French.

Later, we made our way into the Plouescat communal cemetery in a light rain, and found the Commonwealth Graves area where the sailors were buried. The Athabaskan was well known in Plouescat, and had streets named after her, so finding the cemetery was easy.

We entered through a large iron gate that was supported by a stone wall that encompassed the graveyard. To our right was what we were looking for—fifty-one graves of our Canadian sailors, brought to this sanctuary by the residents of Plouescat and lovingly laid to rest the morning after the sinking.

My wife and son placed a Canadian flag on each grave and I, a measured amount of blessed Canadian soil. We said our prayer for them and turned to leave. An older lady who had been watching us honour our dead sailors, approached my eleven year old son, looked up into his eyes and replied, "Je me souviens. " She lovingly stroked his face, spoke to us and told us that she, with her dad, had gone to the seashore with their horse-pulled two-wheeled wagon to help collect the bodies of the seamen that fateful morning, and bring them to the cemetery for burial. At the end of her story she again stroked his face and replied, "Je me souviens" with tears in her eyes.

She had not forgotten these brave men of her youth when reminded on this day by a young Canadian boy who came across the sea to remember the boys from another generation who gave us our freedom.

*"Unlucky Lady", the story of the sinking of H.M.C.S. Athabaskan. Authors: Burrows, Len/Beaudoin, Emile

> *"Don't tell me the moon is shining;*
> *show me the glint of light on broken glass."*
> *~ Anton Chekhov*

Clare McCarthy

Clare is the author of *The Hurleyville Taxi* (*Two Thousand Pounds of Bacon and Bone*), a humorous memoir documenting the life of his late uncle, Howard Hurley, a hog trainer of note. Clare belongs to The Dufferin Circle of Storytellers and contributes a monthly column, *Meandering* as well as a weekly editorial cartoon to *The Orangeville Banner*. In spite of his focus on humour, Clare takes life and writing seriously. His most recent attraction, at the hoary age of 71, is to the El Camino pilgrimage, an 800-kilometre walk through the Pyrenees to Santiago, Spain where he intends to let serendipity be his guide rather than follow a predestined walking plan. Whatever transpires, he hopes to return with a more profound understanding of life and himself, and looks forward to creating further entertaining stories, including photos and drawings of his journey.

UDDER CONFUSION

Doctor Horace Bailey rolled onto his left side and reached toward the clattering phone. Having been a vet for over forty years, he still considered such early morning calls to be one of the biggest pains in his practice. He muttered to himself, "Why the hell does every farmer in Dufferin County figure that just because he's up at five in the morning, the rest of the world should be up as well? Horace reached down with his left hand and his arthritic fingers knocked the jabbering phone off the end table beside the bed. Crashing to the floor, the phone continued its incessant ringing.

"Oh damn, now I'll have to get up to answer the bloody thing." Hoping to avoid having to get out of bed, Horace contorted his body and groped for any part of the infernal ringing instrument on the floor. The more he poked and prodded, the further he had to stretch to reach the phone, but this tortured stretching and straining eventually caused his bulk to crash onto the floor in a cloud of dust.

His wife continued to snore, whistle and wheeze contentedly, in spite of all of the commotion that was taking place around her. Horace figured that any normal sleeper would be wide awake by now, but Dorothy wasn't one of the normal ones. She'd gotten used to his early morning calls and she could sleep through an earthquake. The lousy phone continued to ring—its racket shattering the cave of silence under the bed. Since he was now on the floor, Horace crawled on his hands and knees beneath the bed, through dust mites and balls of fluff, until he cornered his prey against the far wall.

"What the hell is it?" Horace growled into the receiver.

The voice on the other end was unmistakeable. "What's gotten into you Horace?"

"Oh, it's you, Russ. What on earth do you want at such an ungodly hour?"

"Sadie's got a swollen teat, Horace. You're going to have to come out here and do something about it." Sadie of Hillcrest, an ancient Jersey cow belonging to farmer Russell Daley, owner and operator of Jerseydale Farm Dairy, was the oldest patient in Horace's practice. Many years ago, Sadie had won the title "Champion Jersey of the World."

"I'll try to get out to see her sometime this morning Russ, after I shave and have my breakfast."

"Sadie doesn't care if you've shaved or not, Horace, and you don't need breakfast either. Your wife said you're putting on too much weight as it is!"

In exasperation, Horace attempted to end the conversation. "Oh, all right Russ, I'll be out in half an hour."

Russ pleaded, "What can I do for her till you get here, Horace?"

"Soak her teat in a mug of warm tea," Horace advised. That old folk remedy, good or otherwise, would keep Russ occupied until he got there.

"My wife's already suggested that, Horace. I hope you're not going to charge me a whole lot of money for a visit when I can get the same advice from Catherine for free."

"Oh, for heaven's sake, Russ, I've got to hang up or I'll never get out to see you before Christmas!" In spite of the so-called emergency, Horace had a leisurely shave, followed by a substantial breakfast. As he wolfed down two extra sausages with his eggs and toast, he snapped at the sausages, muttering, "You're for Sadie, and you, my lovely, are for Russ."

After breakfast, Horace pulled on his wrinkled old windbreaker and battered fedora. When he hoisted his scruffy leather medical bag from the floor by the door, the effort caused a familiar twinge to dance up and down his lumbar region. He'd been promising Dorothy for years that he would retire, but he continued to procrastinate. Early morning calls such as these, however, pushed him closer to the brink of retirement.

In his driveway, Horace surveyed Old Bertha, the Chevy pickup he'd been using for the past fifteen years. At the purchase of the old girl, Horace requested that a sign painter inscribe on her door the modest motto, "The Best County Vet You Can Get!" With Bertha showing signs of wearing out, her sad condition reflected Horace's own physical condition these days. Horace had made the decision that as long as Old Bertha hung together, he'd continue his practice. They'd go out of business together.

Bertha's passenger door creaked and groaned as Horace hauled it open and tossed his bag onto the front seat. He kept telling himself to ask Irv down at the garage to oil the hinge before it seized up entirely. When the bag landed on the seat, a dislodged puff of dust reminded Horace of the many country roads he'd traveled as a vet during the past forty years.

While the pickup rattled along County Road 23 on its way to Russell's farm, Horace would swear he heard a few more squeaks and rattles that he'd never noticed before. When he arrived at the Daley farm, Russ was waiting, shifting from foot to foot, by the front gate.

"What took you so long Horace? I've managed to milk six cows while waitin' for you to show up!"

No good morning, how are you today, Horace? Just a grumbling, "What took you so long?" Maybe it *was* time to get out of this business. Horace scowled, "Okay, Russ, where is she?"

The vet shuffled to Sadie, and dropped his medical bag close by. "Okaaayyy, Old Girl," he crooned as he examined her swollen member.

"Well, Horace, what do you think? Will she be okay? I hope it isn't contagious."

Horace scratched his left nostril and ran his weathered hand through his shaggy mop of gray hair as he assessed the situation. Catherine Daley had tiptoed into the barn.

"I heard what you said, Russell Daley," Catherine blurted. "The only thing that's contagious around here is your stupidity!"

"What on earth are you talking about?"

Catherine continued, "You realize that this is all your fault, Mr. Daley. If you hadn't forgotten to milk Sadie when you were supposed to on Wednesday, this would never have happened. Her udder was so full yesterday morning, she stepped on her teat, and that's what all this fuss is about."

"Why didn't you tell me that before?" Russ snorted.

"Did you even bother to ask?" Catherine replied innocently.

"I think she's right, Russ. That's pretty well my diagnosis," Horace agreed.

At that admission, Russ grumbled, "An' I suppose you're going to charge me for this visit as well?"

"I'm not in this for the good of my health, Russ, as you can see by the sorry shape of my back. I'll charge you for the antiseptic cream and forget the service call. I'd hate to be responsible for you having a coronary at the sight of the amount if I did!"

Horace returned to his pickup and when he tugged on the door handle, there was a sickening screech and groan from the door's hinges. Horace stood with the door hanging in his hand. "Well, that's it, Russ, this just ruins the rest of my day! Have you got a nail or something I can use to fix that lousy hinge so I can get this ornery contraption back home?"

Russ dug a rusty nail from a box of odds-and-ends in the corner of his shop and, while Horace held the door in position, Russ used a brick to hammer the nail in place of the door's broken hinge pin.

"There'll be no service charge for the nail or my labour, Horace."

"That's mighty generous of you, Russ."

In case the repair didn't last, Horace rolled the window down and tied the loose door to the frame with a scrap of binder twine he'd rescued from the floor of Russell's barn. As soon as Horace pulled into his own driveway, he called Clappison's Wrecking Service to come and retrieve his crippled pickup.

That rusty nail was the last straw and when he walked into the house he hollered, "Well, that's it, Dorothy! Old Bertha's on her way to the scrap yard and Horace Bailey, veterinarian, is no longer in business. Now, maybe my insane life will settle down without some idiot calling at five in the morning to complain about his cow's swollen teat!"

ONE–EYED JACK RIDES AGAIN

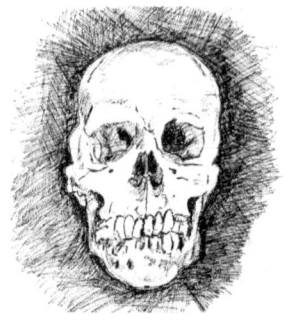

I leaned against the library's pitted brick wall and surveyed the Harleys nuzzling the curbs along both sides of Mill Street, which was blocked off from Broadway down to Little York. Sparkling chromes and gleaming blacks flashed in the bright afternoon sun. A few late arrivals thundered down the centre of Mill, their engines cranked up to a pitch that would not go unnoticed by the other riders nursing a beer, chomping on a burger or having a smoke at the outdoor barbeque set up next to The Four Aces Bar.

Standing alone on the sidewalk was an old guy, well, he'd be at least sixty, I'd guess, with scruffy salt-and-pepper whiskers. His attire contrasted with the sea of leather jackets and helmets worn by other bikers on the street. The old guy sported torn, stained jeans, a wrinkled, red plaid shirt and greasy ball cap. A limp ponytail dangled from his matted gray hair and, if you looked closely, you might be able to distinguish the mousey-brown roots of the hair's original colour from years gone by. This solitary figure exuded the air of a seasoned biker, but showed no signs of taking part in the activities around the tubs of beer and the street-side barbeque. Each time an engine roared —its echo bouncing off the walls—the old guy's right leg would twitch, but otherwise he didn't move. On the surface of his blue tinted sunglasses, I could see a chrome skull with ruby-red eyes reflected from the rear post of the nearest Harley Davidson.

I fell into step behind an unlikely looking pair of cyclists as they ambled down the street, and it was impossible not to eavesdrop on their conversation. Fellow riders addressed the little guy simply as Rat, while his burly companion, wearing a full set of denim overalls, answered to the name Pearly.

Rat squinted sideways at his mate. "Have you seen Jack today, Pearly?"

Pearly's face broke into its usual toothy grin. "Ya, I seen him standin' back there a ways."

Rat shouted over his shoulder at the old guy standing on the sidewalk, "How are ya doin' One Eye? I ain't seen you in a hog's age, har, har, har. Do ya still recall how to tell a happy biker, Jack?"

"Ya, Rat, count the bugs on his teeth. When are you going to get a new joke? That one's so old, it stinks. Jest like you do."

"You remember Pearly, don't you Jack?"

"Yes I do, Rat, but all I know about him is that he's not as dumb as you are."

"Thanks for your vote of confidence, Jack."

Just when the pair was out of Jack's hearing range, I heard Pearly ask, "Why do they call Jack One Eye, Rat?"

Rat shouted back over his shoulder, "Hey Jack! Pearly wants to know why they call you One Eye. Show him, eh?"

"Get lost, Rat, you're gettin' to be a bigger pain in the butt every time I see you."

Rat persisted. "Show him, Jack, I'll even spring you for a jug of suds if ya do." Without waiting for a reply from Jack, Rat headed toward The Four Aces beer table at the end of the street.

Pearly paused, then stepped back onto the sidewalk beside Jack.

"Pearly, you know Rat's as tight as a rat's arse. He still owes me a hundred bucks. I'll consider the beer he's buyin' me to be a down payment, 'cause I'll likely never ever see the rest of that cash."

Rat arrived back, puffing, and handed over the ice-cold brew. "Here's your beer, Jack."

"I'd thank you, Rat, but don't forget, you still owe me that hundred smackeroos." Jack knew that he really had no obligation to fulfill any debt to Rat for the refreshing beer, but he always got a certain amount of pleasure int what he was about to do. He slowly peeled off his sunglasses and dropped them into his shirt pocket. Pearly felt a twitch in his gut as he stared at Jack's weathered face. As a companion to Jack's blue eye on the left, only an ugly empty red socket remained as its partner on the right.

"Get the picture now, Pearly? Rat asked. "Me an' Pearly gotta go down and get some chow, Jack, before them other slobs eat it all, but we might see ya again before we leave."

"I can hardly wait, Rat, but don't sweat it on my account."

As Pearly and Rat continued down the street, I heard Pearly ask Rat about Jack's eye. Rat replied, "Did you never hear about the accident?"

"What accident are you talkin' about, Rat?"

"A coupla years back, Jack was headin' west down old Highway 24 toward Guelph, when he tangled with a transport truck. It was lucky for Jack they was both headin' in the same direction, but unlucky 'cause Jack was barrelin' along faster'n the transport. When I got there, the ambulance boys was peelin' Jack off the back of that big rig. It was just like me scrapin' a great smashed bug off my windshield."

"Gawd," Pearly groaned.

"Jack's right leg was broke in five places, so they had to fuse it all together. Now it's stiffer'n a board. Jack couldn't ride a bike no more, not even to save his grandmother's soul. He comes to these get-togethers to ride again, but it's all in his head. There goes Jack now. I guess he's had his ride for today."

I watched the old guy dragging his crippled leg behind him as he shuffled around the library corner onto Broadway, just past the last of the Harleys lined up on Mill. I couldn't help but notice that Jack was actually smiling.

Alberta Nye

Alberta is a film maker, photographer and part-time writer. As with many people, she feels she has a novel to write that is hidden away amongst her travels and experiences of life that she will one day make into a reality.

She has three children and two grandchildren, a cat named Kolo who came from Hawaii with her, three inspirational writing sisters and a long distance romance that was rekindled after having lost one another for 43 years, which is a novel in itself.

A near death experience at 22 profoundly affected her outlook on life and death. Her latest documentary, *Smiling at Death*, created with the intention of presenting a more positive view on the natural process of death, is in the completion phase. See and read more at www.SpiritValleyPictures.com.

MOMENTS IN TIME

I'm sixty-four but don't feel it. I don't even know how I got to this decade. Time slips and slides and before you know it, years have flown by, in my case, sixty-four of them. I have gathered things along my journey. I carry the scars of relationships lost, the joy of having three wonderful children, the sadness of a failed marriage and the wonder of finding a lost love. I hold close to me memories of ecstatic joy and profound grief.

I have wandered down the halls of Spirituality taking that which has served me and leaving that which didn't. I have opened doors in my life that I wish I hadn't and left some closed that I wish I had explored. I use the knowledge from my past without dwelling on it. I look forward to my future without fearing the end.

Some days I feel eighteen with adventures still ahead of me and other days I feel ninety with every second of my sixty-four years weighing heavily on my back. Some days I am filled with joyous anticipation and, on others, I sit immobile from lack of inspiration or focus.

I usually feel immortal as I did in my twenties, although now that I am in my sixties, realize that I should do those grown-up things like making out a will and sorting through the mementos of my life.

I have lost friends and relations to death. In fact, I have about as many people on the other side of the veil as I do on this side. This, however, doesn't concern me as I talk freely with either side as the mood strikes.

I find I can get away with being just a little more eccentric, although I shall save the best for when I am in my eighties and nineties when I will hopefully get away with even more.

I have a deep appreciation for those I love and want to see them regularly. I hold them a little tighter and a little longer each time we say good-bye. Soon I will be greeting my first grandchild and am eager to swaddle him in my love and support. I look forward to watching him grow and learn the wonders of life and will perhaps smooth out a few of his bumps along the way.

As I always have, I intend to hold the bridle of life and hang on tightly as I make the most of the rest of my ride here. I will love ferociously and live passionately so there will be nothing to regret having left undone when it is my turn to cross the veil.

At least that is my intention.

DEATH VISITS MAGGIE

From this day forward, she would know the smell of death.

Maggie worked in the Royal Hospital in Southport, England as a laboratory technologist. It was a busy hospital and the routine was always the same: draw blood, take it to the lab, test it and report the results to the doctor. This morning would be no different . . . or so she thought.

On that particular day, there were twenty specimens to collect and, as she approached the sixteenth patient, Maggie couldn't help noticing an odour around the man. In her twenty-four years as a lab tech she had never noticed such a smell. It was even affecting her stomach but, ignoring her nausea, Maggie stepped to the bedside, kept her breathing shallow and got to the job as quickly as possible. Mr. Bell was moderately alert and since she didn't want to tarry, she was dismayed when he spoke to her.

"Here's Dracula to take some blood!"

Never heard that one before.

At least you are a pretty one," said the clever Mr. Bell.

"Why thank you, sir," Maggie quipped as she drew the needle swiftly out of his arm. "Now please hold this swab firmly on your arm for a few minutes. We don't want you losing any more blood than necessary and attracting more vampires."

What on earth was that smell? I have to get out of here!

Neither his visitor nor the patient in the next bed seemed to be bothered by the obnoxious odour.

Back in the lab with the tests done, Maggie saw that Mr. Bell had an abnormally high blood sugar and hastened to call his doctor with the results.

Maggie's rounds the next day didn't include Mr. Bell and, when she inquired on the ward, was informed that he had passed during the night. As sorry as she was that a patient had died she was grateful when she went into the ward that there was no remnant of the odour from the day before.

Work carried on as usual and the strange odour drifted from Maggie's memory. She had plenty to fill her thoughts without fussing about such a small thing. Her husband of nineteen years had died six months ago and Maggie was still distracted by her loss. Home was now an empty building where she slept and sometimes ate. Work kept her mind occupied and she knew her job so well that she could do it on automatic. That was apt, as she felt like a rusty robot going through her day.

As time passed, Maggie started to emerge from her fog of grief. On this particular Monday morning, she came to work feeling more cheerful than she had in months. She had gone to Blackpool for the weekend. It was a place where she and Morgan, her late husband, had spent a lot of time. She had almost felt his presence with her as she sat and ate in their favourite restaurant. Maggie wasn't too sure of her beliefs of what happened after death, but something was changing for her as she started to let herself feel as if Morgan was close by. She held that feeling nestled within her as she started her work after the comforting weekend.

The first six draws of the morning had gone routinely, but as she approached the bed of the seventh patient, she was assailed by a repulsive smell and immediately remembered the incident with Mr. Bell. This time the patient was an unconscious woman who didn't stir as the needle slid into her vein. Maggie hurried through the rest of the draws and went back to the lab wondering what the test results would be on Miss Perkins. Could the smell be connected in some way to a high blood sugar? She had drawn for that along with several other tests.

Upon seeing the results, Maggie was a bit surprised. Blood

sugar was normal. Once more she called the doctor with the report and, with a certain amount of disquiet, waited for the next morning to arrive. Would Miss Perkins be on the list of draws?

Morning arrived and Miss Perkins was absent, both in the requisitions and in the bed. Maggie's analytical brain started working. Each day from then on, Maggie kept a booklet with dates, times and test results of patients who had that special smell about them. As part of her research, each time she detected the smell she would approach someone who was in the vicinity.

"Excuse me, but have you smelled anything strange while you have been sitting here with this patient? I think the hospital may be trying out some new cleaners and I wouldn't want it to be upsetting to anyone," she said.

The answer was the same even if worded slightly differently.

"No, I don't smell anything."

"I can't smell anything strange."

"I don't like the smell of his breakfast, but then I hate sausage."

So there it was. Maggie was the only one sensing this odour. *What the heck does this mean?*

The next two weeks brought three patients who died after the warning odour. *There is a connection. This is the smell of death!*

Although it sounded a little ghoulish, Maggie was excited about her discovery and decided to share it with others in the lab. Her fellow lab techs had noticed that Maggie was cheering up and were willing to get caught up in her excitement, if only to support her journey back from debilitating grief.

"Mrs. Winterbottom will be dead by tomorrow morning," she announced to the other techs one day. "And I believe that Mr. Jackson will be gone the day after." She felt bold saying it out loud, but then, she was beginning to feel certain that the odour presaged death and this way she could involve others to be sure that she wasn't just fooling herself.

"What? Are you crazy? Their tests must be through the roof if you can diagnose that accurately," Joan, her good friend, remarked with slight concern in her voice.

"Since when did you become psychic?" called Bob.

"Whacko," someone said from the other side of the room.

Maggie didn't let their remarks bother her. Time would prove her right.

Their remarks changed when, sure enough, Mrs. Winterbottom had died the next morning and the day after that, Mr. Jackson.

Undaunted, Maggie went through her days keeping her list of these special patients.

"Are you okay Maggie?" asked Joan as she saw Maggie scribbling in the small book that she kept in her lab coat pocket. Something strange was going on. Was this connected to Morgan's death in some way? Just when she thought Maggie was beginning to cope, this morbid fascination with death had popped up.

As her predictions became more and more accurate, some of the techs in the lab started to shy away from her. A few were as excited as she and that group would gather to look at test results, and even sometimes arrived early in the morning to see if there was a trend.

This routine continued for several weeks and Maggie became able to predict deaths to within hours. She was a little spooked, but also intrigued with this new ability.

The week before Halloween, five months after Mr. Bell's odour had started it all, two things happened that changed everything.

The first incident involved Mr. Harper, an octogenarian who had been critically ill for three weeks with the same type of cancer that had taken Morgan from her. Everyone in the lab knew it and each day they looked toward Maggie when she returned from the ward. They felt for her and had offered to do that draw, but she insisted that she was all right. They had decided to keep their questions on the playful side since Maggie really did seem to be handling things well.

"So, will it be today?"

"Is Mr. Harper smelly yet?"

"Are you sure your nose is still working?"

"Today isn't his day," Maggie said each day.

Then one afternoon, the inevitable happened. There was the odour as she approached Mr. Harper, and Maggie knew that he would die before morning. "This is it guys," she announced back at the lab. "Mr. Harper's time has come."

Morning arrived and there sat a requisition for Mr. Harper's blood. *What? How could this be?* Maggie gathered her tray and went down to the ward. The curtains were drawn around Mr. Harper's bed. A pale, elderly woman sat nodding off in a chair next to the bed as Maggie quietly entered and approached the bed.

"Oh, good morning, Nurse. I was just resting my eyes. It's been a long night," she said to Maggie.

Because of the white lab coat, Maggie was used to being mistaken for a nurse or doctor, so let it ride.

"I'm sorry to disturb you. I won't be long. I just have to take a little sample of blood and I'll be out of here," she replied.

Maggie reached down and took Mr. Harper's hand to straighten his arm ready for the draw. His emaciated look was so like Morgan's that her heart lurched. *Were those eyes looking at her?* The waxy coolness of his hand slithered up her arm and into her heart. *This man is dead! Oh my God, what do I do now?*

She glanced at the woman by the bed and back to Mr. Harper. His eyes were slightly open and Maggie felt as though she would fall into those narrow slits. *Don't panic. What should I do? What should I do?* Knowing that she had to do something, she grabbed a hematocrit tube from her tray and did a finger stick instead of a putting a needle into his lifeless arm. She squeezed his finger but only a drop of thick blood seeped out and his finger went pure white and flattened. Sheltering this view from his visitor with her body, she quickly gathered her things together. All she wanted to do was get away. Away from the smell, away from the lifeless body that so reminded her of Morgan and away from the exhausted woman looking at her.

"Sorry to have bothered you," Maggie said toward the woman as she turned and left. *I can't look at her or I'll burst into tears.*

The nurse's station was a blur as Maggie rushed past. *I should stop and tell them. I can't. I have to keep going. They'll find out soon enough.*

Maggie paced as she waited for the elevator that would lift her back to safety in the familiar lab. It was one thing to smell death but to touch it again was unbearable.

Back in the lab she sobbed out to her friends what had happened. Joan comforted her as the rest silently drifted back to what they were doing.

The raw wound of losing Morgan had been ripped wide open and Maggie begged him to be there. She needed his touch more than her next breath. She felt a warm hand on her shoulder and turned to acknowledge Joan's support. *What?! Where is she? I know I felt her hand.* No one else was in the room and yet Maggie knew she wasn't alone. Warmth moved down from her shoulder and settled around her heart. *Morgan, is that you?* And yet, she didn't really have to ask. She knew he was with her. *Thank you, my love.*

Maggie eventually made her way back to her work bench to run some tests. She was filled with a strange calm, even though she felt as if she had just survived an avalanche. Dealing with the familiar routine, Maggie hardly had to think. It soothed her back into a sense somewhat resembling normalcy.

The second event occurred at three p.m. when she got a call for an emergency draw on a new patient. They didn't want to wait until morning for the test and Maggie was happy for the distraction. She grabbed her tray once more and went to the ward. Mrs. Smythe sat up in bed and looked the picture of health.

Oh no, not again. "Hello Mrs. Smythe. I'm here to do a quick blood test for Dr. Evans."

"No problem. He just wants me here for the night. I'll be going home tomorrow morning."

Oh no, you won't. "Good, I'm glad to hear that. Lets just draw this blood and I'll leave you to rest."

"No, really. I love visiting and I'm not the least bit tired."

"Maybe I should send around the book lady so you can get a good book," Maggie offered.

Oh my God, why did I say that? She won't have time to finish it! "Okay, all done for now. Good Luck," said Maggie as she grabbed her tray and left the bedside and the familiar smell.

Back in the lab, Maggie was curious to do the testing and talked with Joan while preparing the specimen. She shared how strange it was that this healthy looking woman was going to be dead by the next day.

"Did you day Mrs. Smythe? Is that Sandra Smythe?"

"Yes, I think that's her first name. Why?" Maggie asked.

"Oh no, that's my aunt!" cried Joan as she rushed from the lab.

Maggie was stunned. *What had she done?* She slumped down on her stool at the lab bench and held her head in her hands. Joan was so upset, and Maggie had caused it. What use was this gift?

Enough. This is enough. I don't want it any more. Death comes, but does it have to be announced? Why doesn't everyone smell it? Why me? Morgan, why me?

Maggie finished her testing, called the results and, pleading not feeling well, left for home. She had had enough emotional turmoil for one day. All she wanted was to sit calmly and see if she could sense Morgan there, now that she knew that was possible.

Maggie pulled out onto Main Street and turned toward home, putting on a favourite CD to soothe the fifteen-minute drive. As she reached down to turn the sound up, the smell of death suddenly engulfed her. *Now what? There are no patients within a mile! Morgan? Do you know what is going on? I know you are here, my love, I can feel you.*

Maggie never saw the truck that slammed into her.

The paramedics wondered why on earth this mangled woman would have such a smile on her face.

"Storytelling reveals meaning
without committing the error of defining it."
~ Hannah Arendt

Gloria Nye

Gloria has won several writing awards for her short stories: honourable mention at Eden Mills Writers' Festival, 3rd prize at Words Alive in Sharon, ON, and 1st prize at Elora Writers' Festival, 2010, for *Seventeen Crows*. She has completed two novels and is researching her third in her *Dragonfly* series.

Through Spiral Press (www.spiralpress.ca) she has published *Stories of Prayers & Faith*—a collection of heartwarming and inspiring stories from 26 authors, the *Dream Quest Dictionary* and *A Walk in Fields of Gold: The Headwaters Writers' Guild Anthology of Poems & Prose.*

SEVENTEEN CROWS

Seventeen crows stood waiting at the end of the lane. Yesterday, it was sixteen and the day before that, fifteen. She never believed that crows could count but . . . And were they the same birds each day—plus one—or did new ones fly in just to take turns tormenting her? They weren't even lined up on the split rail fence like respectable crows, but had planted themselves on the hard-packed dirt of the driveway among the scattered gravel that Brad had used to fill in the potholes.

Grandma Stokes always said that crows meant death. Christy never believed that. Why, with the number of crows around that would mean people would be dying every day. She took another step toward the line of black birds.

When the first crow arrived seventeen days ago, Christy didn't make much of it except to wonder why it just stood there on the ground, staring at her. It wasn't pecking on roadkill, or insects or whatever else crows eat and, when she walked past it—only about two feet away—it didn't move. The next day, at half past nine when she went to collect the mail, there were two crows—standing neatly side-by-side, watching her as she walked by. On day three, one more companion had joined them. There they stood, all in a line with marble eyes aimed at her. Maybe they weren't crows. Maybe they were some shape-shifting demon come to harass her. On the fourth day, she rushed the quartet, shooing with her hands and yelling, "Get off now, you black buzzards!" Eight flapping wings lifted the creatures into the air.

When she and Brad moved in two years ago, Brad had put up a brand new postbox well back from the road so the snow plough wouldn't knock it over. He also attached a long skinny pole to it with a Canadian flag on top, so that they could find it when it got plowed under.

Christy folded the flyer around the Bell bill and turned to go back to the house. Those four damn crows had not flown off. They had lined themselves up again and calmly continued to stare at her. With a quick step, she strode past them. All the way to the front porch, she never once looked back.

It wasn't her idea to live in the country. She had come from Halifax to Toronto to be an actress. How could she pursue a career living on 100 acres of farm, miles from nowhere? The small town of Palmerston, ten kilometers away, didn't offer any chance for her to be seen on TV or to get a movie part, but Brad had made his mind up. It was all right for him. As a pharmaceutical salesman—er, representative—he could live anywhere.

She dumped the mail on the coffee table and sidled over to the front window where she pulled the curtain aside an inch and peeked around it. Still there, at the far end of the driveway—seventeen black blobs, forming a dark mass. She yanked the curtain shut, rattling the wooden rings against each other. When would this end? Why were they there? Did Brad hire a crow tamer to drive her crazy? But he couldn't. He was dead, and it wasn't her fault he was killed—not really. She was glad he was gone, but that secret would die with her.

Everyone thought they were the perfect couple. "Perfect" being the defining word. "The roast is undercooked." "You drive too fast." "How many times do I have to tell you to line my socks up from dark to light?"

He would be proud of those damn crows. They came like clockwork and their silence was unnatural. Don't crows squawk a lot? She straightened the calendar knocked askew from the swaying curtain. October 17—six months to the day since the accident. You'd think by now, the letter would have come.

Every morning—not counting weekends—she'd walk down to the mailbox, praying that it had arrived. But instead of a letter, for the last seventeen days, she was met with yet another one of those black creatures waiting for her. Well, she'd had enough. She didn't need eighteen dumb crows staring at her! She spun around and darted to the back kitchen where Brad kept his shotgun. Handy for killing groundhogs and rabbits, he'd said. He'd fancied himself a marksman, but he never hit anything. She picked up the heavy shotgun and slid the shells in the way Brad had taught her.

"I'll give those smug black devils something to think about." She marched out the side door and started down the lane toward the waiting audience.

She had never shot anything before, besides Brad . . . but then, that was an accident, wasn't it? He'd said he wouldn't be back for five days, and he always followed his well-made plans with razor precision. The legal proceedings had taken weeks before she had been declared innocent. Now she only needed the final paperwork so she could sell this place and get back to Toronto to be an actress. No more time to waste. Soon she'd be twenty-five and too old to do anything. She'd met Brad at the *Blue Ginger* where she'd been waitressing between auditions. He looked so crisp and clean and neat, not like the rough Nova Scotian boys. And so what if he was eleven years older than she was? He was established in business and would take good care of her while she was waiting to be discovered. Those first few months were idyllic. Christy loved being looked after and having Brad teach her his sophisticated ways. But he didn't like it when she cut her hair and became a blonde. Then he had the nerve to stop her from taking that movie part. She shouldn't have told him it meant taking off her top. It wasn't long after that when he decided to be a gentleman farmer. Did he think she was stupid? He just wanted her out of the city and away from that man who was going to give her a start in an art film. She had a good figure, why not show it off?

Cradling the rifle across her front, she continued down the drive. It had been forever since her last visit to her Toronto hairdresser and an inch of black roots pushed into her blond curls. The group of crows hadn't moved. It was peculiar how they arranged themselves each morning. You would swear they were giving a math lesson to a bunch of nine year olds. Always in neat groups of twos or threes and then fours. A new addition would patiently stand apart and wait for the next day to be evened up. Just like Brad. Everything had to be in order.

"By whose rules?" she had asked him once.

He looked at her as if she were in kindergarten and said, "Mine."

That night, she rearranged the spices out of alphabetical order, mixed tins of corn and peas in with the peaches and mandarin oranges, and tapped each picture frame—in the whole house—crooked.

So when Brad announced he wouldn't be back for five days, that meant he wouldn't be back for five days. And on Saturday, when they were in town, he told Margie at the L & M Food Market, and Joe at the Esso Station, that he was going to North Bay for five days. So what could a poor girl do when—on the fourth day—she heard someone coming into the house? She had to protect herself. That morning she had loaded the gun and by 8:30 that night, was sitting on the bed waiting. When the figure appeared in the doorway, what could she do but shoot? The recoil of the gun knocked her back on the pillow and the dark figure lay in a bloody heap.

At the trial, she explained that she always took the rifle upstairs when Brad was away, and everyone knew that her husband never changed his plans. She didn't mention that she'd received a voice mail saying he was coming home a day early, or that she had erased the message. But she almost lost it when that good-looking lawyer asked about the call from Brad's cell phone.

"What time did you receive his call?" he asked, glancing down at the phone records, indicating the exact time.

Christy, the distraught widow, shot her eyes skyward, recalling his voice. She had to think fast. Damn those phone records.

"Your husband did call the day before he came home? Unexpectedly?"

"Oh, yes . . . well, no . . . I'm not sure," Christy answered. "I had just started watching TV when the phone rang." That was true. Brad had called on his lunch hour at precisely 1:09, just when *The Bold and the Beautiful* had started after commercials. She looked straight at the cute lawyer. "I didn't answer it and whoever it was didn't leave a message."

It was only a small lie and she was acquitted.

With a firm grasp of the rifle, she continued down the lane, but when she looked up at the congregation ahead, something had changed. Those ornery birds weren't in their neat little rows, columns or groups. As she got closer, she saw they had formed a semicircle with the opening toward her as if inviting her in. She took two steps, and stopped. The group moved as one, closing her into the middle of a perfect circle. The largest bird stretched his neck up and screeched a loud "caw" at her. The one beside it followed with a piercing cry, and the next and the next joined the raucous chorus until seventeen scolding voices had swelled into a maddening choir. A huge bird opposite her—beak hinged wide—spread his wings and lifted off. Christy swung the rifle up in a frantic attempt to aim it. Frenzied shrieks tore the air. Flapping, fluttering wings stormed around her, hitting her face, pulling her hair out by the roots. She shot wildly into the melee, raising a shower of dust and spitting gravel. The rifle slammed back, kicking against her shoulder. She staggered off balance and seventeen screeching black monsters descended.

Old Ted Saunders, on his regular mail delivery, found her the next morning and called 911 from his new cellular telephone. While he was waiting for the O.P.P. to arrive, he put her mail into the box. That morning, he delivered the Sears Fall Catalogue, a flyer for a steel roof that would last a lifetime, and a business envelope from the Ontario Provincial Court with the official announcement of her freedom.

Later that day he was overheard talking to Margie at the L & M Food Market. "She musta been bleedin' out of near to twenty holes, that woman." He shook his head. "Prob'ly all night long."

A CHARACTER OF SUBSTANCE

David turned to the first page of the hardback copy of his favourite mystery writer's latest novel. He hesitated for one delicious moment before plunging in. With a double tap on the metal base of his bedside lamp, he boosted its power to its brightest. He would have at least a good half hour of read before Catherine came to bed, maybe more before she finished examining her latest slew of depositions.

Eager eyes galloped over words, phrases and sentences. Lines turned to paragraphs, paragraphs to pages, while pictures of scenes, characters and settings flowed through his head. Then, halfway down page five, it happened. In less than a nano-second, he was sitting at a long table with the people who had only recently been inhabiting his head.

A virile man of forty-five sat at one end, a gray-haired matriarch at the other. On the man's right, the beautiful Rebecca Saunders reached for a succulent shrimp. She placed it first between two luscious lips, and then, with blood-red finger tips, deposited the tail delicately on the flowered china plate resting between her wine glass and water goblet.

What the . . .? He looked to his left.

A man, vaguely familiar, peered back at him and spoke. "You're a new character," he said. "I didn't expect you to drop in."

"Where am I?"

The man grinned. "Look around."

He looked. Before this bizarre occurrence, he had been reading about this very place: the lavishly set table, the virile man, the matriarch, the bewitching Rebecca Saunders. And there was the stoney-faced attorney opposite him, with the younger auburn-haired daughter on one side and the rebellious nephew on the other. He peered more closely at the company. There was something peculiar about these people. They were barely two inches thick. Only Trevor Saunders, seated imperiously at the head of the table, and the fabulous Rebecca, had any form. She, particularly, was well-filled out.

"These people are cardboard characters," David blurted.

"Oh, be kind," the man on his left said. "You are, after all, only on page five. Give me time to round them out."

An image of the back cover of the book he had just been reading, showing the *Times* review beside a head shot, flashed across his mind. "You . . . you're the author. What are you doing here?"

"I could ask you the same thing." He put a finger to his lips. "Quiet. Something significant is about to happen."

A shot rang out and the gray-haired lady at the far end of the table clutched her bosom, which rapidly turned crimson. Rivulets of red, syrupy liquid squished through wrinkled fingers just before she toppled into her soup. The back of her head consisted of strips of brown corrugated ridges with a scattering of gray wisps poking through. Rebecca screamed, the nephew shouted, bedlam reigned but, in the next instance, David and the author were standing in a dark and quiet hallway.

"Wha . . . where are we?"

"Chapter Two. I like to leave 'em guessing." He turned and charged down the hall.

"Wait for me." David scrambled to keep up with him. The moonlight, filtering through a high oval window, rippled over the edges of a silver picture frame. What was he doing in the middle of a murder scene? Maybe the author had some answers. "So what happens next? Who shot her?"

"Whoa. Not so fast. Anyway, you're not staying. I didn't plan on you turning up."

"Well, what about you? What are you doing here?"

"All authors write themselves in somewhere. Sometimes we shadow our characters or are pieces of them, but, à la Hitchcock, I like to make a cameo appearance."

"But can't I stay? Maybe I could be a detective, or a lawyer."

"Nope, already have those figured out. You just don't fit in,. Besides, you're too skinny."

Just then, they passed a full-length mirror, elongated by its narrow black border. David gasped. He was as thin as tissue paper.

The world jerked, and the hall, the author and the mirror lazily spiraled into a fuzzy mist. He blinked several times.

Catherine stood above him holding his closed book in her hands. The strip of 35-mm film he used as a book mark stuck out the top edge.

"You fell asleep . . . again," she said, putting his book on the side table.

David stared at her as she removed her housecoat—she looked great in that silvery nightgown—and flung it over the chair at the end of the bed. Then she walked to her side and crawled in. Leaning over, she kissed him on the cheek. "Night." She rolled over and pulled the comforter up around her ears.

"The weirdest thing just happened to me."

"Hmmm."

"One moment I was here and then—"

A muffled voice came from under the covers, "Can you tell me in the morning, darling? I'm so tired."

The next day, she was gone when he woke up. He knew when he married Catherine that she had a love affair with her career, but that suited him. He was an independent film maker—at least that's what he had printed on his business cards. So what if he shot birthday parties, graduations and weddings. Someday, he would make a real film.

It was movie Friday. His favourite day of the week. He and Catherine went to the symphony once a month and an art film now and then, both of which he enjoyed, but it was his Friday matinée that he especially relished. Catherine never took a weekday afternoon off, so after a morning of editing, a light lunch and an hour at the gym, he was standing alone at the concession ordering his large, layered-buttered popcorn and a root beer. The 3:20 show at the Galaxy was rarely crowded unless a blockbuster was opening but, even then, he usually got his first row centre seat.

At five to six, he opened the front door, carrying an overflowing, refilled popcorn bag. Catherine teased him about taking it home, but you just couldn't duplicate that movie house flavour.

"Did you forget?" Catherine rushed toward him, dressed in a tight-fitting low-cut black dress.

"Whoa. You look spectacular."

"Never mind that. The Beechman dinner? A very important client? Didn't you get my text? You have twenty minutes to get dressed."

He plunked his gym bag on the floor and popcorn on the hall table. In fifteen minutes, he had showered and dressed in what Catherine had laid out for him and was standing at the front door, tugging at his collar.

"Leave it alone. Stop fidgeting."

"These damn collars are so tight. You know I hate suits. It's just not me."

"Well, pretend for one night. Anyway, you look gorgeous." Her eyes traced him up and down. "Sort of James Bondish."

"You're sort of Holly Go Lightlyish yourself." He reached for her.

She stepped away. "Not now. Later."

"For sure?"

A wicked smile. "For sure."

He dropped Catherine off and continued around the circular drive past the valet service. He didn't even let Catherine drive his vintage T-Bird. After parking in a far corner, he followed the fieldstone path back to the main entrance. Thick lilac bushes perfumed the air, their purple flowers contrasting with two huge snowball trees blooming on each side of an alabaster cupid spurting water. When he reached the front door, he reminded himself to be on his best behaviour and to not loosen his tie until the host did. He hadn't even had the chance to tell Catherine about his dream, or vision, or whatever, from last night.

In the brightly lit checkerboard tiled foyer, a smiling young woman, also attired in black and white, greeted him with a tray of champagne. He took a flute and continued toward the garlanded archway of the main room. Animated voices and lively laughter awaited him. Maybe he would meet an interesting character.

As he walked toward the bustle and buzz of conversation, he passed a full-length mirror on his left. Scrolls and dancing angels festooned the wide gold border. He looked at his reflection and gasped. He was as thin as tissue paper.

Harry Posner

Harry is currently working on his first novel, *Charivari*. He has written film scripts, plays, song lyrics, texts for dance, children's picture books and poetry. His poetry has been published in *Dreamweaver Magazine, Dimensions Magazine, Dining and the Arts Journal* and *Quills*. He has self-published several books, including *The Conscious Scribe: 100 Exercises for the Developing Writer* and *Wordbirds*, a collection of bird poems for young minds. Harry is a member of Words Aloud poetry collective and the Headwaters Writers' Guild. He is active in the Collingwood area, promoting the literary arts through events such as Wordstock: the Collingwood Literary Festival, and his annual multidisciplinary happening—Cyclotron.

Where Did They Go? was a top- ten finisher in the Writers' Union of Canada annual children's writing competition. He lives in the beautiful wilds of Caledon.

WHERE DID THEY GO?

"Obaa-chan." Toshi pushed his nose up against the window. "What are those holes in the snow?"

"They are tracks made by deer, my child."

"Where do the tracks go?"

"Why, they go wherever the deer go."

"But where did the deer go?"

"So many questions." Obaa-chan's dark eyes smiled. "Answers

come when you are ready, Toshi-chan, and right now Obaa-chan is ready for her nap."

"But …?"

"Why don't you go outside and follow the path?" And she padded softly out of the room.

As Toshi put on his coat and boots he heard his grandmother's gentle voice calling, "And be sure to come in before it gets dark."

Outside, Toshi peered down at the deep almond-shaped holes. He decided to follow them.

In the middle of the field the tracks suddenly came to a stop and then… gone, just like that. The snow was smooth as silk as far as the eye could see.

"But, where did they go?"

First, he asked Rabbit, "Usagi-san, where did the deer go?"

Rabbit whispered, "To find out, you must hug the earth." And off she hopped.

"Hug the earth?" Toshi lay face down on the snow and stretched out his arms as far as they would reach. "But my arms aren't long enough."

Toshi searched the entire field but found no more tracks. A carpet of white snow crunched under his boots as he walked.

"Yuki-san, where did the deer go?"

Snow sighed softly, "To find out, you must grow wings."

"Grow wings?" Toshi began to flap his arms. Up and down, up and down, faster and faster. Before long, his arms fell limp at his side. "I'm tired."

But Snow simply lay there, glistening. Toshi scratched his head and watched his breath dance in the wintry air.

Suddenly he heard "Chunchun! Chunchun!" high overhead. A tiny bird gliding through the dusk softly landed on his hat.

"Torí-san, where did the deer go?"

Bird sang sweetly, "To find out, you must catch the light."

"Catch the light?" Toshi could see Obaa-chan's house, now kissed by the rays of the moon. He cupped his hands and ran through a patch of tall, dried grasses, trying to catch the moonbeams as they fell. "It's not working, Tori-san!" But Bird dashed away in a flash of blue feathers.

"Tsuki-san!" he shouted up to Moon. "Where did the deer go?"

Moon hummed dreamily, "To find out, you must grow roots and reach for Heaven."

"Roots? Heaven?" Toshi pressed his feet deep into the snow, then stretched his arms high over his head, reaching for the sky. "Like this?" But Moon fell into a deep sleep.

"Why won't anyone answer my questions?" Toshi stomped toward the edge of the forest. A brisk wind whistled through the branches of a tree so tall it seemed to touch the stars.

"Kí-san, where did the deer go?"

Tree swayed gently. "To find out, you must ride the waves."

"I haven't got a boat!" But Tree stood firm and silent. Toshi frantically paddled his hands through the air. Out of breath, he yelled, "Am I getting closer?"

A splashing sound from the river at the bottom of the hill drew Toshi onward.

He peered into the flowing water and demanded, "Kawa-san, tell me where the deer have gone!"

River burbled tenderly, "To find out, you must seek the drum."

"What drum?" But River rushed away downstream. "What drum? What wings? Just tell me where did the deer go!" Toshi shouted at River and Bird. He kicked Tree and stamped so hard that Snow flew wildly all about him.

Finally, red-faced, Toshi sat down beside River, too tired to shout or think another thought. And all about him became still.

Suddenly, out of the stillness came a sound—*thrum dum, thrum dum, thrum dum.* It was the beating of his heart. For a while, he listened to it and watched River's gentle waves. A ray of moonlight shone through the trees and landed on his boots.

Toshi closed his eyes… and to his wonder two beautiful deer stood before him! They were so near he could hear their breathing. Without a sound they drew closer, and then gracefully bowed their slender heads. Toshi shivered with excitement but remained still, eyes tightly shut. Then, silently, the two deer turned, bounded over the river and vanished. He opened his eyes, but they were gone.

Toshi sprang up and ran back to Obaa-chan as fast as his legs could take him. Over Snow, past Tree and Rabbit, under Moon and Bird, with wings on his feet, he ran and he ran!

"Obaa-chan!" he shouted. "I found them!"

Moon gazed down at the little boy racing across a blanket of sparkling stars, and smiled.

"I love writing. I love the swirl and swing of words as they tangle with human emotions."
~ James Michener

SOCK'S RETURN

"Roobaba, roobaba, roobaba . . . "

Bumped and squished by the damp clothes, Sock and his partner tumbled inside the rumbling dryer.

It's always so dark and hot in here.

A slender hand twisted the dial and the drum spun faster.

"Roobaba, roobaba, roobaba, roobaba..."

I hate it when she does that. I get sooo dizzy.

Sock became a blur of red. *I hope this is over soon. I can't wait to get back onto Grandpa's feeeee...eeeeeet!*

WHOOOP!

Where am I? Where's my partner?

Sock peeled himself off the ground.   Clusters of single socks covered an open field as far as he could see. Bobby socks—green, yellow and blue—slept in loose piles. Hundreds of baby socks, sport socks and fishing socks wandered around in a daze.

A black dress sock with a hole in the big toe slid into view.

"Welcome to Singleton!   I'm the Prime Hose here, made of the finest cotton. I see you've just arrived."

"How did I get here?"

"One minute you're tumbling in the dryer, thinking, 'What a tiresome life,' and the next, whooooop! here you are. That's how we all get here."

Sock flapped back and forth. "Well, I have to go back!"

"Shhh, put a sock in it. You'll wake the knee-hi's. Besides, there is no way back."

"Darn it! I miss my partner, and Grandpa's feet will be cold."

The dress sock leaned in close. He smelled like stale cheese. "You knitted types are always stirring things up."

A crowd of mismatched, sparkly party socks had gathered around. "What's the point of going back?" they shouted. "What have you to look forward to? The minute you shrink in the wash or get a little hole in your toe, they turn you into a sock monkey!"

Sock stood up tall. "But what about the feet? That's why we were made."

A tattered sock covered in yellow ducks shuffled forward. "Feet? Those smelly things. Who needs them? All they do is wear you out."

"Well I don't want to become lazy and useless, like you. I'm going to find a way back!" And with that, Sock stomped off.

He soon reached a forest. The trees were covered with red and blue sport socks snoozing as they swung from the branches.

"What are you hanging around here for?" asked Sock. "Help me find a way back."

"Don't bother. They'll just use you up," replied one of them. "Grab hold of a branch and have a nap."

A sudden wind kicked up, and the lazy socks tumbled around the branches like tired acrobats.

That's it! Sock jumped up and snagged a branch. As the wind picked up, he thought as hard as he could, "I want so much to get home. I want so much to get home!" Sock whirled round and round, pushing with the wind, faster and faster.

I hope this works because I'm getting dizzzzzzz………yyyyyy….
WHOOOOP!

"Roobaba, roobaba, roobaba…"

Sock clung to the cold brick wall behind the dryer. He was back!

Top drawer! Oh, put me on your feet, Grandpa. I miss you so much.

A small hand grabbed Sock. He wriggled as it squeezed him into a dark sack. Lost in a pile of old pants and shirts, Sock was crushed into a ball.

Oh no, what is to become of me? Sock monkey? Christmas stocking? Rag rug?

A flash of familiar red yarn pushed through the jumble of clothes.

"Hey, Partner."

"What? Hmm? Top drawer! It's you!"

"Yes, it's me. Where have you been, you heel? I've been cramped in this bag for a whole week."

"I've been to the other side," Sock whispered, "to where the singles live."

"So what? Grandpa stopped wearing me because you weren't around. And now they've given us both away!"

A pair of wrinkled hands rummaged in the bag and pulled out Sock and then his partner.

Finally, thought Sock.

"These ought to do," a shaky voice announced. "Nice and cozy."

Sock felt the cool skin against his threads. *Smells like cedar. Kind of reminds me of Grandpa.*

"These fit just fine," said the old woman.

Sock snuggled around her toes and sighed. *I'll miss you, Grandpa. But, oh, it's good to be needed.*

THE CASE OF THE SEED THAT WOULDN'T

Night in the forest. For some, a time to hunt. For others, a time to sleep. For the likes of me, Roger Meadowlark, B.I., the night is a nest full of cases waiting to be cracked.

Being a Bird Investigator is not all fun and games. Every now and then, amongst all the open and shut cases, one comes along that makes you shake your tail feathers and sigh. Sammy the Seed was that kind of case.

You see, Sammy grew up in the heart of a kooky kind of sunflower —bright purple. Ever seen one? Neither had I. And Sammy was a pale puny seed squeezed by hundreds of brothers and sisters, all of them fat, shiny and black. No bird worth his weight would want him.

In the end, he was left alone in the heart of a wilting flower, bitter, angry. Sammy hardened up his shell. He became the toughest nut in the field. He wouldn't be cracked.

Hungry crows pecked at him—they'll eat anything. Chipmunks with razor sharp teeth bit down hard on him. Bunnies thumped him with their hind legs. But Sammy would open for no one.

Bertha Blue Jay burst into my tree, hysterical, in tears. "I tried so hard, but he wouldn't crack. You've got to do something, Roger, please!" And she batted those frisky eyes that send a shiver up my crest every time I get a load of them.

"Can't spare the time, too many other cases to solve."

"But he said that even Roger Meadowlark couldn't crack his shell. And he laughed!"

Laughed? Why I oughta . . . Nobody likes being taunted. So off I flew to get the skinny on this upstart seed that refused to play the game.

I soared through the shadows of the forest, keeping my eyes peeled for Sammy. It began to rain—the worst kind of rain—wet. The kind that soaks your feathers until you feel like a lead balloon dragging through the air. I took cover under a huge boulder. Fell asleep right on the spot.

Had a dream. I was a chick, still in the nest, crushed by too many brothers and sisters, the runt of the brood. Last to get fed, last to learn to fly. Hungry, feeling stupid and unloved. And then pushed out, falling through the cold air, helpless. I flapped my wings, but they didn't work. I opened my beak to screech, but nothing came out. I hit the ground, hard!

Woke up with a start. "Stupid dream."

A little shape sitting by the boulder drew my attention. It was a seed—sunflower—and feeling a tad peckish I figured I'd help myself to some dinner.

I tried to crush that seed in my beak. No go. Dropped it from the highest pine in the forest. No go. Soaked it in the lake to soften it up. No go.

"Stupid seed." I began to hop away. Stopped. Whirled around. "You Sammy the Seed?"

He sat there, mute, taunting me with his silence. My tail feathers twitched. He had me ruffled.

"Playing hardball, eh? Okay, Sammy, have it your way."

I called for my secret weapon—Bruiser. The most feared bear in the woods. None too bright, but strong. Those arms could snap a tree trunk in half. He looked from me to the seed and back, hesitating.

I knew Bruiser's weakness. "There's honey in it for you."

Bruiser raised the boulder over his head and roared. Sammy didn't stand a chance. Poor lug. Then I got to thinking. There wasn't a whole lot of difference between Sammy and me. We were both tough nuts, raised the hard way. Shut tight. No love. We deserved better.

"Wait!" I threw my body between Bruiser and the seed. "I can't do it." It was too late. The boulder came crashing down on the both of us! But I was quick. I shoveled Sammy into my beak and took off. The rock smashed to smithereens on the ground behind us. Too close for comfort.

I carried that little seed back to the field he was raised in. Pecked out a nice little bed in the soil and laid him in. "That's okay, Sammy, no law says you have to play the game." Covered him up, nice and cozy. Flew home. Guess you could say I buried the case.

No, being a Bird Investigator is not all fun and games. But it has its perks. "You're just a big old softy," Bertha crooned. "I think you're the cat's meow." She hung around me lots after that. Can't say that I minded.

Summer brought a ton of rain. And the sun was hot, so hot it hung on you like stink on a skunk. The sunflowers grew like crazy. Strange thing, that field that I laid Sammy in…it was filled with sunflowers… every last one of them…bright purple. Go figure.

"If my doctor told me I had only six minutes to live, I wouldn't brood. I'd type a little faster."
~ Isaac Asimov

Len Rich

Award-winning freelance writer/photographer
***1991 recipient - Canada Recreational
Fisheries Award
2007 recipient - OWC Jack Davis
Mentorship Award***
Author of:
Memoirs of a Fly Fisher
So You Want to be an Outfitter
Rivers & Woods
Fly Fishing Tips & Tactics
Newfoundland Salmon Flies ... and How to Tie Them
Best of In The Woods
Tales of Christmas (Editor)
Former **Eastern Director** - Outdoor Writers of Canada
www.lenrich.net

THE SCARECROW

It's not often that you're awakened by the sounds of fire engine sirens when you live on a farm out in the rural areas, or "sticks" as they call them in Nova Scotia, but that's just what happened when Martha was in the midst of a dream about step dancing at a local social event held in the community every year.

She was just about to trip the light fantastic with Carmine the barber, perhaps the most sought-after bachelor in town, when the raucous sounds snapped her from the reverie at the annual Sadie Hawkins Dance and back into reality.

She shook Oscar, her husband of 26 years who was dead to the world beside her in the bed, but all she got in return was a minor groan.

He's got his hearing aids out, she thought. *Deaf as a post without them. Well, now, I wonder what can be burning away out here?*

The flashing red lights of the fire truck were between her and the farm house next door that was owned by her neighbors, Herb and Amanda. Martha's first thought was that Herb had been up to his usual tricks, trying to build a better mousetrap or something that had backfired, but total curiosity caught her in its grip. Despite the early hour and pitch black darkness outside, she just had to see what was going on.

Martha donned a coat over her pajamas, slipped into the old pair of rubber boots that always stood by the back door and, despite the mass of curlers in her hair that looked like a helmet out of a science fiction novel, made her way around the four-acre field that separated the two farmhouses.

By the time she had negotiated her way to the scene of the fire, most of the excitement was over. Amanda was standing on the rim of a blackened ring a good 60 meters across, her arms crossed and obviously not very happy with the situation.

Herb was speaking to a fireman and trying to explain what had happened. His arms were flailing so wildly that Martha expected he could fly if he'd had feathers attached to them.

Amanda touched Martha on the arm, nodded her head toward the house, and gestured to her to come inside. "We might as well have a cup of tea while this dies down," she said, and soon they were seated at the old wooden kitchen table while the kettle boiled.

"What in the world happened?" Martha asked, her natural curiosity now too much to contain.

Amanda poured hot water over the two teabags in the mugs, slid one over to Martha along with the full sugar bowl, and shook her head. This was a reaction Martha had seen many times in the past, and it always meant that one of Herb's experiments was behind it.

"You know that we planted that big field between your house and ours in the spring, right?" she asked. Martha nodded, so she continued.

"Well, things were doing pretty well out there until the crows started coming around, and then the starlings, and God only knows what else started pecking at the corn as they came out. Herb spent most of the day running out into the field to shoo them away, but they'd be back in a few minutes doing more damage. Herb had built a scarecrow to try to keep them off, but they ended up landing on it more often than not, so one could keep a lookout while the others worked their way through the corn.

"Herb figured the old scarecrow wasn't very effective, so he decided to try to improve on it. He had a bunch of old junk out in the shed, a washer motor and some parts left over from a couple of his previous experiments, so he tinkered with it until just before dark yesterday, and by the time we headed to bed he had this new thing rigged up in the field.

'B'Gawd, this'll keep them danged birds away!' he said with a smug smile.

"We turned in and got to sleep, but there was a lightning storm that came through about midnight and the thunder woke me up. Imagine my surprise when I looked out the window and there was the fire burning away out in the field! I made the call to the fire department, and that's what got them out here.

Martha could only nod. She took another sip of her tea and waited for the rest of the explanation.

"Uh huh. You figured it out, I reckon. Herb had that scarecrow rigged so its arms would flap up and down, its eyes would light up, and it would make some sounds like it was the devil hisself out there. And it might have worked, except for the lightning that struck the pole and shot out to the scarecrow. When I saw it last, its eyes were blazing all right, but with real fire, and the arms were going around like a windmill. The sounds coming out of it would scare the bejeebies out of the devil. But at least Herb won't be worried about the crop anymore."

"What do you mean?" asked Martha.

"There's not enough left out there to harvest, the fire got most of it. But it's a real good thing Herb changed his mind and didn't go with his first idea to plant popcorn and sell it to Orville Redenbacher. If he had, we'd be covered in a field of white about this time, and looking for the salt and hot butter. At least that was a blessing," she sighed.

"The two most engaging powers of an author
are to make new things familiar
and familiar things new."
~ Samuel Johnson

Nancy Rorke

Nancy is a founding member of Headwaters Writers' Guild. She has been published in *Stories of Prayers and Faith, The Globe and Mail, Sideroads of Dufferin County, The Top Ten Joy Journal* and *Charting a course for JOYful Living.*

She lives with her husband of forty years, her daughter, granddaughter, three rescued cats, two dogs and a rabbit. One of the cats, a rarely-adopted black one, led Nancy to say, "I believe they find us. It's part of God's plan and we're meant to keep him. His name is Parker, after Spiderman's Peter Parker because one night he got out and stayed lost until a plaintiff meow sounded at the upstairs window. Parker had scaled the wall to the second floor."

THE GIFT

I want to stay in Horning's Mills forever. All my memories are here. If Timothy had listened to me, I wouldn't have to move. The grief of leaving my family has become an overwhelming sadness.

In 1855, when my folks arrived in Melancthon Township from Oakville, the wilderness covered the land and my father cleared it to farm. I was born in 1860, before Dufferin became a county, and I've lived here for forty-one years. Leaving here felt like a death to the only life I'd ever known.

My favourite sister, Georgina lives in Shelburne and we visit often. Jack, my oldest brother lives on the family farm, and the rest of my family lives on farms not far from me.

Little did I know that the series of events that would change my life began with an announcement in the newspaper. On July 12, 1901, there would be an Orangemen's Day celebration that would be the biggest one ever held in this area. The Orangemen had even hired a train to travel from Owen Sound to Shelburne to accommodate all the people who wished to attend.

We hate the Orangemen's Day celebration because we are afraid someone will realize that Timothy is Catholic.

On the morning of July 8, my nerves were on edge. A severe thunderstorm and a disturbing dream had wakened me during the night.

"Timothy, listen to me. I dreamt about the well job that you're doing today for Mr. Jones. I've got a bad feeling. Don't go."

Timothy shook his head.

"Nothing good will come from this."

"STOP, BELLA!   I've spent a lifetime listening to you talk about your dreams. And I've had enough of your damn feelings."

"But last night I dreamt . . ."

"I don't want to hear anything more about your dreams."

"Why won't you listen? I did the cards this morning. I even looked at your cup after you drank, and the leaves say it's bad. You need to stay home."

Timothy stared at the floor.

"Half the town pays me to read their cards and leaves. I've even read for the minister's wife."

"God makes the final decision, not your cards and not the tea leaves."

"My father told me that God offers advice and messages if we just look for them. I was born with 'the gift' and you know it." Tears welled up in my eyes.

"Don't scare me. Hush now. Please don't cry. We need the money. We've been lucky that it has been a dry summer and I have lots of work."

It's strange how a soft voice could come from a six-foot-three man, adored by most women but who, in the end, married me. Walking side by side, we appeared a strange couple with me being five-foot-two. We look almost the same as my grandparents on my father's side.

I often thought about how the strength of our love developed even though neither of our families wanted us to wed because of religion. We fought hard to build a life together.

The tears flowed freely down my cheek. "The bad feeling in the pit of my stomach won't go away." I brushed the strands of my brown hair that had come away from my neatly tied bun.

"If it makes you feel better, I promise I'll be careful today."

I turned away from him, unconvinced. "I'm distraught. The feeling won't leave."

Timothy turned me to face him, and he kissed the top of my forehead to say goodbye. "I've got to go." He turned to the door adding nothing more to ease my fears.

I shook my head at his distrust of my gift.

The problem with having the gift is that I don't know the extent of the damage until after it occurs. All morning, I struggled to get through the laundry. A knock sent a jolt of fear through me. I ran to the door.

Mr. Jones stood on my front porch, clutching his black hat in his hands. He looked at me, unable to talk at first.

"I'm sorry, Mrs. Sullivan. There's been an accident."

I put the palm of my hand up to my mouth to fight back the tears.

"It happened while were digging. I asked Mr. Sullivan if he was going to the big Orangemen's Day celebration and I guess we were both distracted. The large bucket, filled with soil, hung in the air, and it snapped and crashed down on him. It hit him in the head and shoulders. He fell to the ground."

I looked past Mr. Jones to see the men carrying Timothy. I felt faint and the bad feeling nearly overcame me.

Several hours later, when he woke up, he grabbed hold of my arm, and spoke in a low voice, almost a whisper.

"Mr. Jones told me that it felt like death hovered over us. And at first, they believed I'd died. After they checked my breathing, they fetched Dr. Moore."

I kneeled down to his level and stroked his hair. It was worse than I'd imagined.

"Bella, I can no longer do physical work. We're going to have to move to the city."

I shook my head in disbelief.

"I'm sorry," he said.

"The train will cost a fortune. How will we take the cedar chest that you built for me?" I sighed. "It's a wedding present."

"We can only take what we need."

"I'm a country girl. I'll never fit in with city folks. And who will tend Annie's grave? Who will put flowers on my mother's grave and my grandmother's? What about my herbs and my ability to heal? You know my family can't afford a doctor."

"I have no answers. You're the one with the gift."

"I've told you before. The gift is to help others. Sometimes, I'm lucky knowing our future, but it almost never happens."

"Maybe if we lived in Toronto, Annie might have lived. I swear the winter of '84 killed her."

I glared. Annie was my beloved first child. "Don't use Annie to convince me."

"If there was a way to stay, I would find it. Trust me, it's the best for all of us to move."

I started to weep.

"All your tears won't help us and are a waste of time."

A week before we were to leave I sat down with the youngest children before bedtime.

"Mama, am I allowed to bring Teddy?" Gertrude asked.

I smiled and nodded.

"How about my wagon that daddy built for me?" little Timothy asked hopefully.

"I'm sorry, Timmy. The wagon can't come." He slumped down in his seat. I looked at Gladys playing at my feet.

"We're taking Pearl and Blanche. Right, Mama?" Gertrude said.

"Of course."

The older children, Maude, Hatt, Thomas and Bert were all packed to go. They hid their feelings, but I could tell they were upset.

Timothy viewed the move as a big adventure. His family, the Sullivans, were from Newmarket, and he wouldn't miss Horning's Mills like I would.

A few days before leaving, I visited my father on the family farm for the last time. I stood at the screened door and watched my father. Since my mother's death, his youthful appearance had faded as he sunk into the role of widower. Now gray and tired, he remained mostly mute, preferring silence.

He led me into the parlour and closed the door. He turned to me and I understood that something important would occur. I hoped that he had some money from his meager savings to help us.

He appeared somber as he kissed me on the top of my head, showing his grief at losing his favourite daughter. He knew that we'd exchange letters and that I wouldn't be returning. Sometimes the gift can be a curse to endure.

"Isabella," he said. "I have something to give you and it is more precious than gold to me. My mother gave me this before she died and I'm bestowing it to you. You, in turn, must pass it down to one of your sons or grandsons. It passes from female to male, to female and then male again."

"I don't understand," I said, raising my right eyebrow.

"For hundreds of years, this charm has been handed down from our ancestors."

I held out my hand and expected him to hand it over.

He smiled. "No, this is a charm of words, held in secrecy. People will pay money for it. It cures warts. Imagine, in this day and age that there is a cure for it. Remember when I cured Jack's warts on this feet and the relief that he felt?"

I nodded my head and my father continued.

"You may charge money for those that have lots to spare, but for our family and the poor, you must provide the service for free."

I kissed my father on the cheek before leaving. I knew he'd blessed me by acknowledging the gift we both shared. I'd earn a small amount of money from the charm, and I could always do readings to help us.

September 3rd was the day that I left my birthplace and grief overwhelmed me. Jack took us to Shelburne to catch the train. If I'd been born the oldest male, I would have had the family farm instead of the gift.

Desperate waves of sorrow washed over me. There was no escaping as it followed me everywhere and reminded me of my loss. Melancholy and sleepless nights had drained me and kept me quiet. If only Timothy had listened to me and hadn't been hurt.

Before stepping on the train, I glanced at my father and brother. This would be our last goodbye. There were tears in my father's eyes. The air surrounded us, and it felt as if a blanket of sorrow wrapped me in loneliness and despair.

It seemed as if time stopped while they disappeared from sight. It felt like a timeless sequence of events that had occurred beyond my control. I wiped the tears away from the corner of my eyes, and a tide of anguish settled in my heart.

"We'll come back, Bella," Timothy promised. "It's only for a short while."

I nodded. I didn't tell him about the dream that I had last night.

I dreamt that we'd die in Toronto, and I'd never see my family or my home again. But my great-granddaughter will find her way to Dufferin County and my home. She will carry the gift.

She'd arrive in the hot July sun of 1981, eighty years after our departure. It would take her twenty more years, but she'd stand on the hill of the cemetery in Horning's Mills. She'd plant a pink rose bush on my mother's and father's grave. She'd find my journal and she would then write about the summer of 1901 and of me, and I would live again in blessed Dufferin County, if only for the moment.

Based on a true story, previously published in *SideRoads of Dufferin County*. My great-grandparents, Isabella and Timothy Sullivan left Horning's Mills in the early 1900's, after my great-grandfather had an accident while digging a well. Isabella's parents and her grandmother are buried in Horning's Mills.

METAPHORS OF YOUR LIFE

Everything is confusing.
I don't know the truth of my existence.
Reality seems illusive, hidden from view.
What meaning have I assigned to this saga?
Could I not make another choice and change my life?

I cannot see a clear path, nothing appears to be what I imagined.
Is life nothing but a fantasy? O, the Maya that I live in.
Does it matter what my truth is?

How can I find myself in this confusion?
Am I in a metamorphoic state, waiting to discover myself?
Should I fly away like a butterfly or am I the dream?
Is symbolism lurking in the background?

My soul whispers to me, "All is not lost.
Walk away from the chaos and the confusion.
I shower you with messages from heaven above.
Symbols are everywhere and are my gift to you.
Life is but a dream . . . interpret the metaphors of your life like a
dream.
Decipher it and realize the encoded secret, hidden from view.
Life, like a butterfly requires metamorphosis."

Jayne E. Self

Orangeville, freelance writer, Jayne E. Self is passionate about mysteries. Her first novel, *Murder in Hum Harbour: A Seaglaglass Mystery*, will be released in October 2011. She is also a contributing author in the best selling anthology, *A Second Cup of Hot Apple Cider.* Jayne is a member of Headwaters Writers Guild, The Word Guild, and Crime Writers of Canada. You can find more of Jayne's short stories, articles and blog at www.jayneself.com

THE LAST APPLE PIE

"It's not our responsibility, Mother," said Sharon. "We paid the church ladies to make Dad's funeral luncheon and that includes the pies."

Seventy-one year old Eleanor Graham hoisted the flour container onto her kitchen counter, like she'd done so often during the forty-seven years she and Bob had been married. This was the last apple pie she'd ever make for Bob, and no matter what her daughter said, Eleanor would do this last thing.

She blinked back tears. "The church ladies never make their pies the way your father likes. How can I let him go without his favourite pie?" Eleanor handed her granddaughter, Bree the basket of apples.

Bree plunked it on the table. "It's not like he's going to taste it, Grams."

Undeterred, Eleanor scooped flour into her largest yellow ware bowl. "They always use Cortlands. Your grandfather never liked

Cortlands." She added a dash of salt to the flour. "And they don't make pastry the way he liked either."

Bree's cell phone chirped and she stepped into the hallway. Her latest boyfriend called every hour, unlike Sharon's husband, Richard who'd stayed in the city. Perhaps that was why Sharon seemed so irritable.

Sharon pushed the apples aside. "I don't see how baking a pie matters now, Mother. There are so many other things that need doing before Dad's funeral. He'll never know the difference."

Eleanor bowed her head, hiding her hurt Sharon's sharp words caused, and concentrated on blending the lard with the flour. She overheard Bree in the hallway.

"No, I'm not into funerals, Jake, but Mom says I have to stay and help with all the stuff that needs doing. Right now we're making Gramps his last pie."

Eleanor shrank further into her grief. It sounded so irrational, the way Bree said it. She bit her quivering lip. Why couldn't they understand she needed to say good-bye to Bob in her own way?

"You and Bree don't need to hang around if you have someplace else you need to be," she told Sharon. "I'll be fine by myself."

Bree slid her cell phone into her jeans' pocket as she strolled back into the kitchen. "No, I'll stay. Jake's just feeling left out."

Sharon tied one of Eleanor's gingham aprons around her waist and began wiping the countertop with a damp cloth.

Eleanor sighed. "I haven't met Jake yet, have I? Is he coming to the funeral?"

"Trust me, Mother," Sharon said. "You'd remember this one if you'd met him."

Bree lifted the lid to the sugar canister. "Right. Pick on Jake day."

"Is he a hockey player, like your last boyfriend?" Eleanor asked.

"Jake's in a band, Grams," said Bree. She dipped her moistened finger into the sugar, then licked it.

Eleanor almost smiled as she watched. Bree tried so hard to act adult but in moments like this, Eleanor still saw the little girl in her. "Jake's a musician?"

"He's a punker," said Sharon. Her mouth pursed when she said "punker," as if she'd bitten into a grapefruit.

"At least he cares enough to call and see how I am," Bree said.

Sharon bristled. "Meaning?"

Eleanor closed her eyes. *Please don't let them turn the afternoon into a battle.*

"Would you mind doing the apples, Sharon?" she asked and handed her the paring knife. "The sooner we get this pie into the oven, the sooner you can get home to Richard." Sharon's husband was too busy to help with funeral arrangements. Or perhaps Sharon had told him he wasn't needed.

Bree's eyebrows rose. "Hasn't Mom told you?"

"Told me what?" Eleanor looked from her granddaughter to her daughter.

Turning her back, Sharon rifled through the kitchen drawers. "Mother, where's the apple corer I gave you for Christmas? I'd rather use it than your knife."

Sharon was forever giving her kitchen gadgets. Eleanor didn't have the heart to tell her she'd never used them.

Bree said, "Why don't we each make a pie for Gramps?"

Sharon glanced over her shoulder. "You mean each of us make our own pastry?"

"No, we'll use Grams' pastry. It's always the best, but we can make three pies. One'll be from you, one from me and one from Grams."

Stainless steel apple corer in hand, Sharon slammed the third drawer shut with her knee. "You're saying your grandmother's pastry is better than mine?"

Bree winked at Eleanor. "You asked," she said with a shrug.

Sharon scowled. She had no sense of humour and Eleanor knew that was one of the reasons Sharon's first marriage failed.

"I make my pastry exactly the way Mother taught me," Sharon said as she scratched off the corer's sticky label. "How you can say mine is different?"

Bree picked through the apples, selected the rosiest and polished it against her pant leg. "The last time you made a pie, I was in, what, grade six? The crust was tougher than Jake's guitar case."

Sharon snatched the apple out of Bree's hand. "You remember a pie I made ten years ago?" She pressed the corer through the fruit as easily as a hot knife through butter.

Eleanor stared as Sharon peeled each perfect wedge and Bree grabbed a second apple.

"How many pies have you made since?" Bree asked.

Eleanor said, "We're just about ready for those apples, dear."

Ignoring her, Sharon dipped each apple slices into a dish of lemon juice. "I've been busy. I work for a living, remember? I have a career to maintain. I don't have the same luxury Mother did. I can't stay home and bake all day."

Eleanor turned the finished pastry onto her pastry board, dividing it into three mounds. Bob had made this board the first year they were married and she'd been rolling her pie dough on it ever since. She stroked the stained wood with floury fingers.

"It wasn't luxury, Sharon," Eleanor said. "It was hard work. It meant doing without and struggling to make ends meet." She picked up the paring knife.

Sharon shifted sideways, making room for her. "I wasn't implying you didn't work hard, Mother, I simply meant life is different now. Our expectations are higher."

Eleanor winced. "Your father and I may not have had fancy holidays or new cars, but we lived happily together for forty-seven years."

Sharon hammered the corer through another apple. "Every time we're together, you drag up my divorce. Does it make you happy, parading my failures like that?"

Eleanor stilled. "I never meant to make you think you'd failed. It's just your father and I wanted the best for you."

"And staying married to Frank was best?"

Eleanor studied her daughter's pale face. "Has Richard made you any happier?"

Sharon glared back at her. "Now you're after Richard too?"

"I'm not trying to pick a fight," Eleanor said.

Bree reached between them and snagged an apple segment. She dipped it in cinnamon sugar and popped it into her mouth. "Don't take it personally, Grams. She's pissed about everything since Richard's asked for a divorce."

The paring knife clattered to the floor as Eleanor pressed her hand to her heart. On top of everything else, this seemed too much to bear. She wanted to reach out and hug Sharon but she knew her daughter would stiffen and pull away. So like Bob, Sharon checked her deepest emotions tightly inside.

"Sharon, honey, I'm so sorry," Eleanor said.

Sharon wordlessly scattered flour on the counter and, taking one of the pastry mounds, pounded it flat, grinding in flour.

Eleanor nudged the flour bin out of Sharon's reach. "Not so hard."

Sharon pushed out her elbows. "I know how to make a pie, Mother."

Beside Sharon, Bree mixed cinnamon sugar with the flour on her section of the counter.

Sharon said, "The pastry's already too rich. It doesn't need sugar."

Bree grabbed a handful of cinnamon sugar and scattered it over her pastry as she rolled it flat.

Sharon clamped the lid on the sugar canister. "With an attitude like that, it's no wonder you have nothing but heartaches."

Bree shrugged. "I bet Richard wouldn't be asking for a divorce if you sweetened *your* pie a little more."

"Bree!" Eleanor's hand bumped the dish of lemon juice, sending a stream of pale liquid across the counter. She reached for the cloth to mop it up.

"It's true, Grams. Richard's been stepping out with his sweet, young assistant while Mom keeps her nose to the boring old grind stone. Not me, though, I tell you. I am going to enjoy my life."

Shoulders sagging, Eleanor folded her pastry and fitted it onto the Pyrex pie plate. How had it all come to this? She'd tried so hard to live a good life, be a good wife, a good mother. She wanted Sharon to learn from her example, the way she'd learned from her mother. Instead, Sharon had grown hard-hearted, callous. Where had she gone wrong?

Engulfed in miserable thoughts, Eleanor filled the pie crust with apples, dusted it with sugar. She cut the extra pastry into strips, then dabbed them with egg whites and wove the pie's lattice top. A pie top full of holes.

Bree, meanwhile, heaped sugar, apples and cinnamon onto her thick bottom crust. She rolled a second pastry circle for the pie's lid and plopped it unceremoniously atop the fruit.

Sharon frowned at Bree's finished pie. "It's going to boil over. These apples are too juicy *and* you overfilled the pie shell."

Bree lifted her chin. "At least it will taste good."

Eleanor wanted to scream. Why couldn't they get along—at least for today? Couldn't they see how important making this last pie was to her? "Please, girls," she begged, "Gramps so hated it when you argued."

Sharon squished her pastry back into a ball and began again. "No he didn't, Mother. It's only you who gets upset."

Eleanor fisted her trembling hands. "Then, for my sake will you please try and get along? Here, Bree, slice the pie top in a few places and add this." She rummaged through the cupboards till she found a bag of uncooked macaroni and handed Bree one elbow shaped pasta. "It's like a chimney and maybe your pie won't boil over as badly."

"It'll let out the steam," Sharon said as Bree stabbed the macaroni in place.

If only they had a macaroni chimney. For two agonizing years they'd watched Bob suffer through radiation treatments, chemotherapy and countless hospitalizations. Now Eleanor struggled to hold herself together. Did Sharon and Bree feel the strain too? Were Bree's sugar fixation and Sharon's angry battle with her pastry their ways of coping?

Silently, Eleanor watched Sharon rework her pastry for the dozenth time before she finally rolled out the pie shell. She arranged the perfect apple slices in a spiral, sprinkled them with sweetener, cinnamon and corn starch. And, as Sharon lifted the pie top into place, Eleanor held her tongue and her breath, praying the crumbling crust would hold together until Sharon finished laboriously crimping the edges.

Without comment, Eleanor slid the three pies into the oven, slipping a cookie sheet underneath Bree's—just in case. Closing the oven, Eleanor glanced at the kitchen door. She kept expecting Bob to walk into the room and say, "Eleanor, my love, you make the best pies in the county. But don't you think I should taste test this one to make sure?"

Bree must have read her thoughts. "Do you think he's watching us?"

Eleanor said nothing as she dropped the apple cores and peels into the trash.

Sharon said, "I know you think Dad's with Jesus, Mother, but I believe he lives on in our memory, not heaven."

Like so many other things, Sharon's lack of faith grieved Eleanor. "Is that why you agreed to make the pie?" she asked.

Sharon paused while untying her apron. "Maybe. And because you needed to do it, your way of saying good-bye."

Tears pricked Eleanor's eyes. She wrapped her arms around Sharon, "Thank you."

Soon the pie crusts would rise. The scent of bubbling apples and spice would fill the kitchen. Hadn't Reverend Miles said something last week about prayers rising to heaven like incense? She held Sharon tight. Maybe this last apple pie was about more than good-bye.

Caitlin Smith

Caitlin enjoys the creative process and explores all types of writing from short and long stories to poems, anecdotes, travel pieces and even prosaic items such as newsletters and marketing materials.

She is a registered Spiritual Psychotherapist with the Canadian Examining Board of Health Care Practitioners and is a Reiki Master and Teacher. She believes that it is through exploring the interconnectedness of body, mind and spirit and respecting the power of conscious, caring communication that we support transformation and she tries to bring this philosophy to her writing. She currently lives in the Orangeville area, sharing a house with Megan, her best friend of over thirty years; Emma and Nathan, two very pampered cats; and Samson, whom she describes as a truly splendid Pomeranian.

GOD IS IN MY BATHROOM

The first time God performed a miracle in my life, I was up to my armpit in a toilet tank. It was one of those bitterly cold February evenings in mid 1980's Toronto—the kind of night where the frigid air freezes the hair in your nose and gives you ice-cream headaches. I had just returned to my second floor bachelor apartment from a Brownie meeting. The church where we conducted the meetings was a forty-five minute bus drive away and I was cold and tired and ready to spend the rest of the evening sitting on the couch wrapped up in a warm blanket, sipping on a mug of hot chocolate.

I changed into my nightgown in the tiny hallway between the bathroom and kitchen that doubled as my dressing room. While putting my clothes away in the closet outside the bathroom door, I was distracted by the sound of running water coming from the toilet. Over the last few days, the noise had been steadily growing worse and I had been meaning to speak to the superintendent about it.

Curious, I entered the bathroom and stood on the chilly tiles, staring down at the toilet as if it were going to magically tell me what was wrong. Now, I am not a woman who asks people to fix things for me. I am one of those, maybe-I-can-fix-it-myself, how-hard-can-it-be people. MacGyver, but without the scientific training. Sometimes, I can figure something out and I am justly proud of myself. Sometimes, as in the case of the antique clock my mother gave me which stopped chiming, there is a SPRONG sound of rapidly unwinding metal and the clock goes in the garbage.

I took the lid off and laid it on the edge of the bathtub, then looked inside the tank.

The first thing I noticed was that the arm that held the float, instead of being at a 90-degree angle, was slanting down toward 45 degrees while an arc of water streamed out of the fastening for the arm, over the armature and splashed down into the reservoir tank.

With no premonition of the catastrophe I was about to unleash, I reached out and, with two fingers, pulled the arm and the float back up to its normal 90-degree angle.

All hell broke loose. The entire armature: the float ball and arm, the lever, the chain, the stopper—the whole shebang—came away in my hand and a torrent of water blasted out of the tank to the ceiling.

In seconds, I was soaked to my skin and a river of water was pouring out of the bathroom into the little hallway and over to the main room carpet.

Instinctively, I plunged my right arm down into the toilet reservoir and held my hand flat against the surge. The icy cold water pushed against my hand and arm, frothing around me and trying to escape to paint the ceiling again.

I don't know a lot about toilets, but I do know that they come with a shut-off valve. I looked down and, fortunately, it was on the same side I was facing so, with my left hand, I stretched down under the tank to the knob.

I gave it my all, but the knob wouldn't budge. Desperately, I tried again and again until my hand was raw from the ridges of the stubbornly jammed metal.

My palm started to bleed and I looked around urgently for something I could use to protect it so I could keep trying to shut the water off. The toilet roll was soaked and all the towels were in a cupboard in my little hall.

From this eye level, I could clearly see the ceramic walls inside the toilet tank and noticed a stamp proudly proclaiming "Made in Canada, 1955" which, I was afraid, meant that no one had touched this toilet in a good thirty years and that nothing short of a first-rate plumber's wrench was going to turn this obstinate cog.

Blinking back the tears, I took stock of my situation.

My right knee on the toilet seat supported most of my weight, my bare left foot on the cold, wet tiles strained to keep my balance while my right arm remained buried in the tank, keeping the water from becoming a fountain to the ceiling again. Hair and nightgown were sopping wet, and I noticed that my soaked cotton nightgown was now completely transparent. Cold toilet water that had pooled on the ceiling began dripping down on me in big, fat, drops.

Miserably, I considered my options. I did not have the building superintendent's phone number readily available. Looking it up in the phonebook would mean taking my hand away and allowing the gushing water to flood my apartment and possibly the one below. A frantic dash down to his apartment in my soaked (and now see-through) nightgown would be worse, and taking the time to change was out of the question.

Calling out for help wouldn't necessarily work as I was the last apartment on my floor and the connecting wall to my neighbour was the furthest wall away from the room in which I was now trapped. Also, my door was locked with the chain on and this was before cell phone days as well.

Frantically, I tried to turn the knob again but with my palm puffy and oozing with ripped and raw skin, I could only use my fingers, a move which was completely ineffective on the seized knob.

What do you do when all your options are exhausted?

My right hand and arm were numb from the ice-cold water which would occasionally escape to shower me with arctic toilet water. My shoulders were burning, the knee on the toilet seat aching, and my left foot on the cold and wet tiles began slipping. My injured left hand was red and throbbing and no longer able to grip the handle to the shut off valve, let alone turn it. What other choice did I have except to let the water flood my apartment while I went to get help?

I prayed.

I'm not sure "praying" is the right word. It certainly wasn't like any other prayer I had ever made. No, "Hi God, It's me. Could you please . . ." or any of the mutter-along-with-everyone prayers you learned in Sunday school or church.

No. In my desperation it was a direct to God declaration, no ego, no couching in pretty words or phrases, no bargains, not even begging. Nothing but two words.

"Help me!" Not so much a request as a command. A simple acknowledgement that God was the only being around who could help me, and that I needed that help right now.

I leaned down and put the fingertips of my aching, wounded hand on the unyielding knob and tried one last time. It turned. Easily, as if it had been turned on and off every day for thirty years. The water slowed, then stopped and the crisis passed.

Much later, after I had cleaned up, warmed up, bandaged my hand, changed into dry clothes, spread towels on the floor, called the superintendent and was finally sitting on the couch wrapped in a warm blanket and sipping on a brandy—the time for hot chocolate long past —I considered that stubbornly stuck knob.

Did I manage to dislodge it before I prayed? I couldn't see how I had. My hand was truly injured, and my strength sapped from repeated straining. I would have felt the knob turn if I had been able to jar it loose before I gave up.

Then it hit me. Maybe that's the way God works. Not an angel flying in to the rescue. No storms of light and blaring of trumpets. No more turning water into wine. Maybe these days, God answers our yells for help with whispers. Whispers that work, but leave the door open for us to wonder. If you don't want to believe, you don't have to. If you want to believe, here I am.

I don't remember if I even said thank you after this event. If not, I'm saying it now. Thank you, God. For on that night, God was in the bathroom with me and helped me when I needed it most.

I have tried to re-create that moment of Divine connection with varying degrees of success but I guess God knows that I am one of those maybe-I-can-fix-it-myself, how-hard-can-it-be MacGyver women . . . at least most of the time.

ORIGINAL SIN

What would happen if your inner six-year old self could speak with you?

I'm so glad to meet you; I'm just six years old
I'm really quite special (or so I've been told)
I like to play marbles, or swing from a tree
I'm bright, like an angel, so valued and free

I played on the playground, in the bright morning sun
I laughed and I ran, I skipped and had fun
Then, a cold shadow passed me—the day lost its glow
As a stranger appeared, walking painfully slow

Her eyes had no sparkle, her face was just flat
And she was incredibly, horribly fat
Her soul had black holes, like a block of Swiss cheese
And she cowered beside me, then dropped to her knees

She wanted to hold me, she tried hard to smile
She said that she'd just like to talk for a while
Then, I saw the thing
She was scared I would see
That this big, wounded woman was who I would be

I looked through the grayness, looked right in the pain
Saw how she'd been damaged again and again
Then I did something awful (least I felt that I did)
'Cause I really felt sad for her, so she went and hid

"Don't look, please don't see me, and don't see what's been done
"To the angel you once were, you beautiful one
"You were precious and loving, full of promise and light
"But soon you will live through long years of dark night"

She turned from me blindly, didn't see me reach out
She felt dirty and ugly, full of mourning and doubt
I knew she was crying as she lumbered away
And I desperately wanted to ask her to stay

But she wouldn't look at me—like my glow hurt her bad
And it pained her and shamed her that I felt so sad
She saw me as Christ-like, with an innocent glow
And to know that I'd die soon was, to her, a great blow

I reached out my arms but she just ran away
So I stood on that playground with nothing to say
Won't you tell her that it is okay to come home?
That she doesn't have to leave me out here all alone?

I know that she's dirty and that she's been shamed
I know that before me is a dark road of pain
Tell her I'm in here waiting while she's out in the cold
I'd tell her myself, but I'm just six years old.

SLEEPING BEAUTY'S LAMENT

Do not storm my castle walls
Do not hear my mournful cries
Though each day I'm trapped in solitude
My poor soul shrinks and dies

Do not brave the wicked thorns
Do not leap the deadly moat
Though deep inside my dark despair
There lies still a shred of hope

Do not listen to my cries
Of deep torment and pain
Because the master torturer
And the victim are the same

The siren's call, "Help me!"
And the wicked villain's laugh
Come from the same throat, don't you see
The victim . . . and her other half

Now, my beauty's buried deep
And my charm has lost its glow
And though inside, I mourn its loss
I know it had to go

If you think you see a shred
Of the one I used to be
Do not try to bring it out
Or you'll get the worst of me

I'll defend my castle walls
With my fingers in the flames
I'll defeat you if I must
And I'll sadly take the blame

Let's not talk of battles won
Or sigh for beauty lost
For these thick and deadly walls
Were built at quite a cost

Inside these jagged walls
I have built a place of peace
Safe inside, I'm all alone
And I have signed a lifetime lease

"I'm not a very good writer,
but I'm an excellent rewriter."
~ James Michener

GIRL IN THE BOX

She lives in the box quite unhappily
Full of dark, liquid pain and fragility
What does she think on, what does she see?
Is every day still the same, is there no clarity?

In the box, there is no sensuality
There is only cruel, dark sexuality
She is stuck in the past in captivity
Reliving those nights of brutality

Can you hear my voice, girl?
Do you want to be free?
Can you open the box?
Can you run out to me?
Girl in the box, don't stay lost in old times
Come out of the box and see the sun shine

Let go of the past and come up to the now
If you listen to me, I will show you how
Take the image that's burning a hole in your mind
Then imagine a door closing slowly behind

See? The door is quite real and the pictures so dark
Have now moved to the past (though they've still left their mark)
You are living right now in the new century
And the past is the past, and now, you're set free

Tell me your story, I'll listen to you
Then it's time to move on, that's what we need to do
It's time to climb out of the dark box of fear
And see you're okay and you're still living here

Do you want to play now? Do you want to be loved?
Do you want to recapture the times that were shoved
Out of your time and lost in the haze
Do you want to play in some pleasant sweet days?

Go play on the swings or go ride a bike
Leave the past in my care. Go and do what you like
Be free, go and fly—run, jump—swim like a fish
Laugh at old jokes, play the games you have missed

You're not bad, you're not evil, not mad or a fool
You're an innocent kid who went through a harsh school
And you learned a few lessons you would rather have missed
But there were good lessons too—you've become wisdom kissed

It's your time now, to go do what you want
The past has moved on now, there's nothing to haunt
Think of love, think of kindness and sweet mystery
It's for you. It will happen. Just you wait and see

Be kind to yourself now, and I'll be kind, too
For you're part of me and I'm part of you
So together we're moving and free of the past
Closed the door on the blackness—moved forward at last

I reach out my arms; hold you safe to my heart
Now, please, come inside; fill that lost empty part
Girl from the box with me, standing as one
The darkness is over, the future's begun

*"A writer's mind seems to be situated partly
in the solar plexus and partly in the head."
~ Ethel Wilson*

Ed Wildman

The late Ed Wildman inspired and mentored a small group of writers. This group, spearheaded by Nancy Rorke, formed the Headwaters Writers' Guild. Our bi-weekly meetings are based on his workshops that he taught in Honeywood, Ontario.

In the words of his friend, Tom Bryson, "Ed always returned to his avocation (and sometimes vocation) of writing despite the interruptions and distractions of a family and his 33-year old career of practicing law."

Ed wrote prose, plays and poetry. The poetry featured here is from his published book, *Gentlemen of the Street*, reprinted with permission from the Estate of Ed Wildman.

We miss you, Ed.

ED'S EYES

Ed's eyes,
in the rearview mirror,
looking back on a life
spent observing the honesty of people
willing to lay themselves on the line,
doing time, which,
eventually and inevitably,
does them.

VISIT WITH DOCTOR FRYE

Three years after I graduated from Victoria College,
without honours for reasons that are about to become obvious,
I decided—God knows why—to attend Osgoode Hall Law School,
"where it then was," poor neighbour to the Ontario Court of Appeal
on Queen Street.

I needed a reference from a professor.
I went looking for Kenneth McLean.
I had loved the way he squirmed
when he read his beloved New England friends,
Hawthorne, Melville and Emerson,
but he was summering on Walden Pond with Henry David Thoreau
and I was ushered into the overwhelming presence of Northrop Frye.

"I took your first year English class, sir," I began bravely.
"But I haven't taught a first year-class in years," he replied,
"What authors did we study?"

The question disabled me.

At that moment, I couldn't remember one, not a single one,
not Swift, not Pope, not even Dryden or Blake.
And I sat there in critical silence as he wrote:
"I am sure Mr. Wildman can do
whatever is required of him at Osgoode Hall,
Sincerely, Northrop Frye."
And I accepted it with gratitude, except perhaps the sincerity part,
that part did raise a judicial doubt
in my beginner's mind.

SUNDAY AFTERNOON HELLO

I'm saying hello today.
Hello to the solitary white blossom on my Chinese Lily
and to the three tiny sprouts on the yellow cactus in my kitchen,
the desert's hope in microcosm.

I'm saying hello this afternoon
to the excitement of Frances' newest and most powerful landscape
as I listen to Doris McCarthy suggesting:
"Do your work and let someone else worry about how good it is."
I'm thinking about Bruce Powe's solitary outlaws
and Lewis Lapham's admonition about our wish for kings.

I'm saying hello this afternoon
to the brilliant primary colours—reds, blues, yellows—
and yes to the pinks as well,
especially of the Mexican folk art Frances brought back
from Tarpon Springs in Florida.
Spunky, funky spirits
reminding me of distant drums in Taos, New Mexico
And Larry's explanation that silence is the drummer's hardest rhythm.

I'm saying hello this afternoon
to my self, my elusive self,
the one I need to discover before it is too late.
I know I am one of a kind but I must find out—

What kind?

ANCIENT RHYTHMS

In that marvellous old house in Cornwall
the upstairs apartment was empty.
I remember the shining hardwood floors,
the dormer windows with their ancient bevelled glass.

Mrs. McIntyre let me play my alto saxophone there
in an alcove where the echoes surrounded me.
It didn't matter that I only knew one song:
"I'm in the mood for love."

I remember Mrs. McIntyre's hands,
frail and so graceful,
playing accompaniment in a rhythm of their own,
a modulated voice speaking of days gone by.

I remember those hands
as I watch Levon Helm's hands,
moving like two hip butterflies in unison
in the sound studio in Woodstock, New York,
when he sang backup for his old friend, Ronnie Hawkins,
and their song too was of "Days Gone By."

Judy Zarowny

In her teaching career, Judy facilitated student writing in high school drama classes. When her son Matthew died she began writing journals to get through the long grieving period. During that time, she wrote and produced a play, *Burying Grandmother*, about a family coping with the death of a beloved family member.

She is presently finishing a work of creative non-fiction—a book of short stories which she hopes will bring comfort to others who have lost a child to suicide. Drama has two masks—tragedy and comedy. While enduring the tragedy, Judy finds relief in writing comedic poetry and lighthearted essays. The Ottawa South Community Association Review (OSCAR) has published one such article: *The Bank of Paper Bag* under the *Tasty Tidbits from the Trillium Bakery* series. Like her son, Judy is also a visual artist, expressing herself through drawing, painting and photography. She wishes to thank her family and Headwaters Writers' Guild for their unflagging support.

THE FRIDGE

Oh fridge, blessed shrine to those of us,
who, being empty, seek fulfilment
and come to worship at your chilly
fortress of contentment.
What mystery lies within your belly,
oh, well spring of nourishment,
queller of angst?

What delights beckon behind your stainless steel handle,
your face, festooned with hummingbird and daisy magnets,
paper treasures from a child's hand, jokes on
yellowed newsprint, announcements of sales, soirees past
and a gallery of lists recounting groceries to buy,
guests to invite, tasks to-do, promises to make, wishes
yet to manifest
poetic notations, humble testament to life's moments
stacked one upon another till they exceed the weight
a hummingbird can hold.

Ah, fridge.
Many times a day, I come
to court you, seeking to improve my mood
wishing there was a two-headed dog with saucer eyes
forbidding my entry, demanding I perform
some life-threatening test before I am allowed to
partake of your bounty.
Alas, you are easily breached, your door yielding to my touch,
in a flood of light, illuminating your treasure laid bare.
My eyes prowl in lustful scrutiny searching out
the victim to sacrifice upon the alter of my
addiction.
Food.
Luscious, tongue teasing, lip smacking,
mouth watering, finger sticky, food.
crunchy, creamy, slippery, spicy,
tangy, salty, bitter, sweet,
greasy, oily, fat mouth-flattering food.

My restless fingers search for the exact
morsel which will quiet fears that fester
in my soul and whisper worthless
While hand to mouth I plug the holes that never fill.

My teeth butcher the left-over fowl
nesting in a pungent velvet sauce
and tear the cool sweet flesh from
watermelon rind. Next, the cake I ravage
plunging urgent fingers into icing
exploding, melting in my mouth
in peppermint and chocolate ecstasy.

My body's filling up, expanding,
momentarily at rest.
But then my mind goes rummaging
through memories, restless and yearning
tempting me back to treasures of the tongue.
And in my absence, fridge, you call to me
seductively with promises
of peace, fulfilment, satisfaction.
And I return to probe the bottom
of your bowels in search of deeper meaning
But find cast-off delights of sweeter times
secured in glass, transformed
by delicately veined webs of
blues and greens, putrid in their poison;
or hopeless grapes, forgotten,
languishing in plastic bags, weeping;
or, the remains of once splendid feasts
now moribund in Tupperware.

Oh fridge, you hold a promise undelivered.
The rot-revealing underbelly of our affair
has left me burdened with the heavy
weight of my indiscretion.
I vow to end this blubbering, this cellulite
accumulation of illusion and obsession
I'll tear the amusements from your face,

the hummingbirds and daisies
and all frivolity they support
and make you stark and unadorned.
I'll clean you out in every corner
leaving you the empty one!
I'll place with care the treasure that I put in you
and I will be the two-headed dog with saucer eyes
that keeps me from your siren song
and I will be the master of my mouth, my mind,
my body and my life.

"If I fall asleep with a pen in my hand,
don't remove it.
I might be writing in my dreams."
~Terri Guillemets

THE VOICE

I open my eyes cautiously, sit up and push the bed covers back. So far, all is quiet. *I get it. This morning it's waiting for me to make the first move. Okay, here goes:* "What will I wear today?" I'm sitting on the edge of the bed, staring into my closet. "Let me see: I like the black pants and vest with the white blouse."

"Bad choice," says the Voice. "The pant legs are too wide. Makes you look fat."

"Well, well, you're here bright and early."

"Of course I'm here. I'm always here."

"What about the black skirt?"

"Too tight around the waist, accentuates your stomach."

"Well, what then? I can't sit here all day. Is there anything in that closet that doesn't make me look fat?"

"Probably not. You shouldn't eat peanut butter and crackers after dinner. Then you wouldn't have a problem."

"Oh shut up," I say, stepping into the shower, still wondering—no—now worrying about what to wear to work.

"Look at you," says the Voice.

"I'm looking," I say. "I can see that I have grown a few sizes."

"You look awful! Don't look in the mirror, and make sure you wrap yourself in the over-sized bath towel. You should do something about that."

"I go to the gym twice a week, and take long walks with Dog."

Dog, waiting loyally on the bath mat, perks up with the mention of his name, and greets me with a furry dance and ecstatic whines as I step out of the bathtub like I've been gone for three weeks.

"See? Dog loves me. Dog doesn't look at the outer me, Dog doesn't even mind seeing me naked; Dog sees the beauty of my inner self."

"Dog . . . is hungry," says the Voice, rolling my eyeballs up into their sockets.

"So, I'll go to the gym four times a week. I'll go on a diet. No, an un-diet. I'll eat—well, maybe mostly—raw food."

"Ha! You'll never stick to it."

"I could try being a vegetarian again."

"Didn't work last time."

"Or become a Vegan. Michelle did that and the weight fell off her. She looks like a million dollars in her new wardrobe. How I would love a new wardrobe."

"That'll never happen."

"Will you shut up?"

"Face it, the accumulation and distribution of fat in the aging body is hereditary. You're starting to look like your mother."

"Not everyone's distribution of body fat is hereditary," I say, pulling on underwear and surveying my ample bread basket and not so boodelicious derriere. "But, you're right." A feeling of despair has oozed into my words. "I do look like Mother!"

"What did I tell you?"

Dog is now pushing his food dish around the kitchen floor with his nose. The Voice continues its needling while I measure out the same dry pellets into the dish, noting that Dog doesn't need any mayo, ketchup or a side of fries to send him into a frenzy of writhing and yodeling in anticipation of his meal.

"Ah yes, simple plain fare," says the Voice. "Too bad you didn't stick to that. But it's too late for you now; you've already packed on the family weight."

"So what if I do look like Mother. Mother was a wonderful woman. Everybody loved her. Dad adored her."

"Your dad . . . was hungry, and he needed his laundry done and his shirts ironed."

"That was a low blow," I say, stretching the fabric to close the fastener on the black pants. "Dad was loyal and loving, and all those rumors about an affair were not true. You are evil and malicious and slanderous."

"Uh uh, mind your temper. You're losing control. You know that's why John left you—left you for that sweet young fitness instructor. That, of course, and your inability to keep a place tidy. Tidiness is next to godliness!"

"That's cleanliness is next to godliness, you sanctimonious idiot, and I am clean! You are a parasitical, bog-trotting muckworm and I've had enough of you." I button up the white blouse with a vengeance. "You're waiting to ambush me every morning even before I get out of bed, reminding me of the stupid things I said and did the day before, tormenting me with my shortcomings, my lack of intelligence, self-esteem and competence. I feel depressed and defeated before I even leave the house in the morning."

"I'm not ambushing or tormenting you. I'm looking after you. I'm keeping you from falling into the same traps that have hurt you in the past."

"Not!"

"I'm protecting you from embarrassment, keeping you safe."

"Safe?

I'm your guardian angel, the wise one who is a compilation of all the voices who have ever looked after you, taught you, manipulated you, loved you or had your best interests at heart."

"Gimme a break."

"I have years of experience in looking after you, which makes me eminently qualified to do so."

"Well here's a news flash, super nanny . . . I'm not happy."

"Who said anything about happy? I'm just doing my job."

"Your job! Is that all this is to you, a JOB? I want to be happy, and you're making me miserable. You're making me sick. I have high blood pressure, depression, anxiety, 'the misery of psoriasis,' irritable bowel syndrome and falling hair. I can't make a decision, I'm fearful, and I can't move forward in my life with you nagging me all the time. This is my body and I want you out. You're fired!"

"You can't fire me."

"Oh yes I can."

"No, you can't."

"Can!"

"Can't."

A rush of bottled-up rage rips through my belly and out the top of my head in a blast of steam. "Okay, then! You've been tearing me up, and tearing me down all my life. I've come to the end of my rope! I am going to exterminate you. I am going to rub you out!"

I grab the Voice by the throat and started slugging. Bif! Bop! Slam! Boink! Soc! I jump on the Voice. Pounce, pounce, pounce! Pummel! Kick! Stomp! Pounce! Then I take out my mega-caliber, gigantic bad-ass Rambo incinerating rapid-fire attack weapon and, Blam! Blam! Blam! Blam! I put an end to the Voice.

Dog flails his legs on the newly laid laminated look-a-like hardwood floor till they dig in, and he shoots out of the kitchen, through the hall and sails into the bedroom on the scatter rug, where he remains, cowering under the bed. I collapse on the floor, exhausted, wiping the sweat from my face with the black vest, grateful for the silence.

"You don't have to kill me to get rid of me, you know."

"Arrgggh!"

"Just give me another job."

"What?'

"Give me another job."

"What do you mean another job?"

"You gave me this one."

"I did not. I would never give a job to a venomous, censorious, vitriolic, deprecating, spleeny, onion-eyed moldwarp like you!"

"You wrote my script."

"I never wrote your script! You said that you were a compilation of all the voices that had ever influenced me."

"Yes but you integrated all that fault-picking, fear-mongering, libelous foul-mouthed cynicism, into the angry, self-deprecating, fear ridden, goal squashing, joy-killing character that is me. You wrote the script. I simply deliver it."

"Deliver? HA. You batter me with it."

"I am a conscientious employee and I do my job well."

"But I would never say such abusive and disparaging things to anybody, let alone myself."

"So write me a new script."

"That's it?"

"That's it."

"Whoa. It's going to take a lot of work to get this turned around. But wait, I'll get to spend time thinking about and writing down all the good qualities I see in myself."

"Right."

"I'll get to appreciate my body just the way it is."

"Uh huh."

"And my accomplishments—I'll get to feel satisfied about them. And I'll get to love my imagination and be grateful for my talents, my friends, my job—I'll get to celebrate the small victories I experience every day, and think about ways to appreciate my family and my co-workers . . ."

"You're on a roll."

"Then, I'll mull it all over, and you'll repeat it ad nauseum, because that's what you do, and I'll create some more positive thoughts, and you'll repeat those back to me . . . and on and on and on."

"Sounds like a plan."

"Wow! I think I'm going to love this!"

"Me too."

After dinner that evening, Dog cuddles up beside me and my laptop, on the sofa. "Dog knew all along that I was wonderful," I say. "I am going to base our script on Dog's vision of my true inner beauty, creativity and kindness. Dog sees only the best in me. How simple and uncomplicated is that?"

"Brilliant," says the Voice.

"But first, I'll finish this sparkling little piece we're writing."

"Good idea. And, by the way, the black pants and slightly wrinkled vest look quite slimming on us."

"Thank you."

"Now, about the buttered popcorn we're eating . . ."

My eyes fly open, my muscles tense up and I inhale with an audible whooshing sound.

"What about it?"

The silence is palpable.

". . . It's delicious," says the Voice.

FLATULENCE
(From "Fat and Other F Words")

When somber mood lies heavy, silence reigns,
this raucous fool with foul intension looms.
Disrupts, unmasks, embarrasses, defames,
in mirthful exhalation, empties rooms.
It gurgles round in amplified chagrin
from chapel pews in pent up pressure strong;
In hymns, released in odorific din,
escapes in unison on sacred song.
It struggles to release its foul emission
when lovers' words of passion are caressing,
or when lawyers fling their phrases of suspicion,
and kings with presidents their laws addressing.

    Wherever drones the elevated word,
    a fart is sure to render it absurd.

"To me, the greatest pleasure of writing
is not what it's about,
but the inner music the words make."
~ Truman Capote